Father Away From Me

When a Child's Heart is Broken by an Absent Dad

RICK ROGERS

Contents

Introduction

"Father Away from Me" is more than just a book about how difficult it is for children to grow up without a dad at home or in their lives. It is a heart-wrenching saga of the lasting impact that is felt when a father leaves, and how much pain a family suffers due to the absence of a committed father. These pages will take each reader on a tour of what it's like to miss out on having that all-important dad around to support a healthy transition from childhood to adolescence, and on into adulthood. Although the overall perspective is from a boy's view, there will be times when the effect of abandonment by a father on little girls' lives will be considered as well.

Because of the gaps and cultural shifts between our yesteryears and present years, the dedication to fatherhood is not taken as seriously as it should be. No doubt this topic may have exhausted itself throughout the generations via books, documentaries, church sermons, etc.; yet I am confident that this approach will find its way into the souls of persons across uncharted landscapes and territories, while managing to provide a topical relief until the Lord's healing touch closes the wound.

When Jesus uttered the words, "It is finished" from a rugged, blood-drenched cross, He was also saying, "I love you" through His torturous suffering, as He delivered the world from the bondage of every kind of physical and emotional pain. What might this have to do with a topic about absent dads? The human side of God (incarnate) might have felt abandoned for a moment when He cried

out,
"...My God, My God, why have You forsaken Me?" Mark 15:34 (NKJV)

So, He truly understands, and has compassion for children who hurt as they journey through life without a father. [Important to add that the Son was not deserted by the Father. Rather, it was the sin of the entire world that was taken on by the Son that prompted the Father to turn away.]

In as much as Jesus' suffering and separation was necessary for the sake of our salvation, He still empathizes with the sufferings and aftereffects we experience in this life.

In *Father Away from Me* I invite everyone to come along for a field trip that I trust will deliver hope to those who are longing to retire from the aches and pains caused by dad's empty seat at the dinner table. At times it may even stir emotions which may have fallen into a state of complacency over the years. The various details of our scripts are certain to differ, but common feelings will probably intersect at similar crossroads along the way. When they do, let's pause to reflect, but forge ahead with brighter expectations. I am confident that doing so will play a huge part in not only bringing closure, but it will also open that "stained" glass window and let some refreshing air into our stagnant enclosures.

What's oddly exciting about this literary endeavor is that I feel a new sense of freedom about being transparent, and I believe that it will launch a trifold objective: ultimate deliverance and recovery from my own plight; inspiration for those who have been deprived of having a dad, and wholesome motivation for men who are (or will become) fathers. In every case, the achievement of an even greater goal is to encourage everyone to seek after a stronger relationship with our **Heavenly** Father.

Regardless of how it may appear on the surface, *Father Away from Me* is about forgiveness, restoration, and reconciliation. Its pages are a narrative by design, but its message offers a glimpse of the brightest days imaginable.

The challenge for anyone who settles into this story is to resist the temptation to allow anger or resentment to take center stage. Instead, believe that "...**all** things [not some things] work together for good to those who love God, to those who are called according to *His* purpose." Romans 8:28 (NKJV)

This verse can be accentuated by meditating on it in reverse: *"Since God created me, He has a purpose for me. For this, He blessed me enough to be called to a purpose that glorifies God, proclaims His sovereignty and causes me to love Him deeply. And, since I love Him, **everything** works together for the good of His overall plan for my life and for the advancement of His Kingdom."*

In addition, this book will enlighten you about the struggles that a mom faces while trying to play the role of two parents. You'll recognize her as a familiar hero who works hard at attempting to fill the gap. She is always there and at all costs; perhaps not always exactly like the Proverbs 31 woman that the Bible describes, but certainly worthy of an honorable mention. You will find her story here too, from the happy, enchanting days of a promising relationship to the shocking realities of coping with fading interests and the devastation of desertion. As hurtful as it is, her story must be told also.

Father Away from Me is compelling, convicting, and comforting at the same time. It is structured to be a multi-faceted slant that pushes behavioral speculations to the side and brings more reasonable summations into focus. The search for dad might be an expedition that may be thought of as being a bit too late in the game to embark on, but the search for peace and true joy is still attainable and rewarding.

Dedications

To the best Father that anyone could ever have - He is my Heavenly Father, the God of Abraham, Isaac, and Jacob. This book is my "drum" and I play it for You as an offering of praise and thanksgiving. You have been with me every step of life's journey, and I thank you for giving me an opportunity to serve You through the words of this book.

***

I dedicate this book to three incredible ladies: my wife, Cathy, my mom, Elaine, and my sister, Denise. All three have been strong women of faith and have raised their children in fatherless homes. Their dedication to nurturing their kids is the epitome of a mother's love. You have my deepest love and respect, and I thank God for blessing me with an everlasting connection with you.

1

<hr>

A "Rude" Awakening

WHAM!!! SCREECH!!! WHAM!!! CRASH!!!

Our protagonist fell asleep behind the wheel and was smashed **into** consciousness by a guardrail, a skid across a four-lane interstate highway, and a median divider before finally flipping upside down into oncoming traffic! The forceful impact of an approaching car put a halt to the ensuing traffic, but not before fleeting images of an unstoppable 18-wheeler would enter his mind.

Motionless—yet aware—he gently whispers, "Jesus, help me."

If there was ever such a thing as inexplicable calm during a moment when panic should rule, it was then. Instead, silence; an eerie stillness in the night air unmeasured by time. The hush was broken by the sound of running footsteps followed by the shattering of glass. All at once, I (yes, I) was pulled by both arms and dragged from the vehicle to a safe distance in order to be out of range from what could have been an explosion. In no time there were sirens, flashing lights, and concerned faces looking down at me. I was lifted onto a stretcher while an oxygen mask was put on my face as rapid-fire questions designed to test my cognizance came my way. I remember thinking that unless I'm in a state of shock and can't feel the full extent of my injuries, I must have made it through.

The experience that was unfolding was harrowing, but my view of the sky as I laid there was not only breathtaking; it was also soothing, almost as if I was supposed to interpret something from it. I can't honestly say that God's voice was as clear as the starry sky above, but there was no doubt of a message tugging at me during the ambulance ride on my way to the hospital. However, the backdrop of medical trauma all around me for the remainder of the night distracted me from being able to attend to the message being conveyed in a divine way. That would come later. For now, I was probed, tested, squeezed, and questioned until I was given the okay to leave sometime around 2am the next morning.

The doctor called it "lucky," but I knew better. All I walked away with was a tiny scratch on my forehead, while the stranger who dragged me from the car sustained bloody lacerations on his arms from breaking the window to rescue me. I was so grateful for his heroism and I was happy to be able to contact him shortly thereafter to express my thankfulness personally.

Needless to say, the SUV was totaled. What's more, after seeing the remains of it at the place it was towed, I am SO glad that I had no sleeping passenger next to me since that compartment was completely caved in. Driver's side? Intact. In the days that followed, much time was spent replaying the incident over and over in my mind. When I came to the part when I calmly asked the Lord to help me, the "light" went on. Not only did He grant that request, but the hidden message also blazed into focus. He did, in fact, help me, so that I can help others. He had something for me, while also having something for me to **do**. I am called to edify and encourage the men of this world to recognize the lasting impact that fatherhood (or the absence of it) has had on family and society.

What might that have in common with a near-fatal accident on a winter night in 2005? Damage. But, despite the times we're living in as redefinitions run rampant, there is still a great need for a deeper understanding of a father's role.

Here's hoping and believing that an uncanny revival in the hearts of men throughout the land will occur, and that order within the home will bring about a return to an era when honorable fathers were a welcomed commodity.

The Trophy of Trust

One Friday evening more than 20 years ago, I attended a men's conference at a church in Poughkeepsie, New York. There were several speakers who taught on various themes that were all power-packed with encouragement and scriptural insights. Among the group of speakers was a pastor who explained carefully the importance of a son receiving his father's trust as he grows into a man. From a biblical perspective, he took us through the relationships between Abraham and Isaac; Isaac and Jacob, and Jacob and Joseph. (These accounts can be found in the book of Genesis.) To understand how divinely special it was to be trusted by your father, is to be aware that to **not** receive his trust was more like a curse. So glad that's a thing of the past. Or is it?

He brought us more up-to-date by proclaiming how fortunate he was to have his dad present at all times and mentioned how his happiness was directly associated with the trust, affirmation, love, and guidance from a father who gave of himself freely.

He went on to share with us a couple of examples:

1. When he was 11 years old, he and his dad were working together to repair his grandmother's leaky roof. At that age he was certainly without the skill to do it on his own but he was still confident that he could be a good helper because he'd be learning from the best. Suddenly, his father got called away to some sort of emergency and turned the task completely

over to him to finish alone. Doubt in himself and fear of messing things up became the bug in his ear, until his dad assured him that he believed in him and trusted him to do his best. With such a boost of confidence he went on to do just that, and it turned out to be a great job!

2. Next, he told us that as a teenager it became traditional for his dad to give him the car keys after church service every Sunday so that he could take his girlfriend out for a Coke. One Sunday the son got into a wreck and did serious damage to the car. I don't remember how long it took to get it repaired, but as soon as it was, something incredible happened. After church, the son was walking out the door with his girlfriend when his dad stopped him and asked where he was going. He replied, "We're going for our Coke." At that point without any hesitation, his dad tossed him the car keys. He explained to us how he was not only shocked, but that he felt so blessed at the same time.

What an overwhelming display of trust and forgiveness! With such solid groundwork that was layered with abundant lessons from an amazing father, it was no wonder why he became such a powerful man of God and a dynamic teacher of the Word!

The next portion of his message set the stage for an altar call like I had never experienced before. He assured us that although he was privileged to have flourished in a household with a father who blessed his every effort, his heart was broken for the men in that sanctuary whose fathers were absent from their lives and/or didn't gift their sons with the same upbringing. Knowing that we were out there, he did the unexpected. He beckoned us to rise courageously from our seats and make our way to the altar so that he and the other pastors present could pray over us for healing.

"Don't even think about it," he said. "Just come."

Nervously and reluctantly, I stood and went forward slowly. Then he uttered something that struck a chord in all of us.

He said, "Some of you are tearing up even as you come forward."

Now, why did he have to go ahead and say that? I went from tearing up while walking, to crying once I reached the altar, to bawling when a pastor hugged me like a long-lost son returning home. I can say honestly that I had never cried that hard before that moment, nor have I done so to this day! That was like a dam breaking at the seams of every point of emptiness. What was surprising is that I knew I was hurting, but I didn't realize that my pain was deep-rooted. What was even more startling was that the semi-circular altar was quite large, and the men that formed a chorus of weeping "orphans" were more than I could count. We were a group of adult men who turned into a giant puddle of weeping little boys that night. No longer were we able to hold that beachball under the water.

The opportunity blind-sided us, and we were rendered helpless to our bottled-up emotions. So very relieving, but so very tragic at the same time. Unfortunately, I believe that many of us walked away having flushed out suppressed emotions, but we would be lying to ourselves if we felt that the pain was left behind at that altar. It should have been, but it wasn't. Instead, it was a finger bandage over a heart wound. That all-too-familiar saying, "Time heals all wounds" was written incorrectly. Time doesn't heal all wounds; it only conceals them better. (I will be exploring this topic later.) My guess is that some form of follow-up counselling would have been a very good idea.

Coded Men

Sadly, this kind of confession and open display of sentiments hasn't been very popular in our society throughout the decades. Men are supposed to be tough, resilient, "Mr. Spock" type of creatures. We're supposed to shake it off, suck it up, and stomp it out. Our framework calls for the dynamics of a machine that will never break down—especially in front of people. The call is for us to go through life resisting help in most situations such as medical attention, directions when we're lost (ladies, stop laughing), or physical tasks that require more than one person to tackle. Check out this true story...

I was walking through my apartment complex a long time ago when I noticed a man trying to move an oversized sofa by himself. He had it standing up vertically and was twisting and rocking it back and forth as he inched it along the walkway. To make matters worse, he had no dolly or furniture pads to prevent it from being scuffed up by the concrete. His pregnant lady was walking helplessly beside him and appeared frustrated until I approached and asked him if I could give him a hand.

Surprisingly—but then, not—he said, "No thanks, I got it." Although they were strangers to me, his woman looked at me with a facial expression that said, "If you don't grab the other end of this sofa, I'm going to whip both of you right here on this sidewalk, pregnant and all!" She didn't utter a word, but I heard her loud and clear!

After he put the sofa down horizontally on the sidewalk, I took hold of my end, and we carried it to his apartment building. What was even more shocking was that we then had to lift it up a flight of stairs to the 2nd floor. Now how in the world was he going to do that next phase by himself when he couldn't even manage to get it to the building? Probably the same way I would have. Without any help.

Don't want it, don't need it. Yeah, right!

That's how we roll, especially when we are lacking in wisdom, which should be added to the list of other dad-instilled attributes influenced by a strong patriarch. Without him leading, loving, edifying, trusting, and encouraging, we are susceptible to being drawn into society-driven delusions regarding manhood. Oh, we might figure it out eventually, but we'll more than likely end up like that damaged sofa by the time we arrive.

Like Father, Like Son

Along with the special care from a devoted father comes the reward of ripe fruit. That son is now ready to start the cycle all over again when he has a family of his own. Things will not always be perfect, but there will be a sense of warmth and security within the home that creates a genuine atmosphere of completeness. Without it, there will be more bumps in the road of life than needed.

****Dads, please see it as a tremendous privilege to experience fatherhood. The biological portion of it is nothing short of a blessing and a miracle designed by the God of all creation, while the dutiful part of it should compel every father to honor God by raising his children in the same loving way that our Heavenly Father nurtures us.*

After He began His covenant with Abraham, God said in Genesis 12:2 (NIV): "I will make you into a great nation and I will bless you; I will make your name great, and you will be a blessing." And, **that** he was. Likewise, was his son, Isaac. Genesis 26:3-5 describes the blessings from God that he earned because of his father's obedience. Then, in Genesis 27:28-29 the pattern continues with Jacob, followed by his 12 sons (especially Joseph), and the beat goes on throughout history. Got time for one more amazing true story before moving on?

2020 was an extremely difficult year. Not just due to the onslaught of the Covid19 dilemma, but because my church family received the devastating news that our lead pastor's beloved wife was stricken with breast cancer. Our love for her and her family created a wave of prayers and support that extended beyond our immediate surroundings and as far off as Ukraine and other remote places abroad. Within a matter of months, healing and remission ushered in a time of excitement when Pastor Kelvin and Amy set out for what turned out to be a seven-week road trip across the country to enjoy beautiful sights and major landmarks. Such a wonderful way to celebrate better health, marriage, and a renewed appreciation for life! When they returned, they remained guarded as the pandemic was still making its rounds and attacking at random. Nevertheless, we were all so happy to have them home and optimistic about the prospect of her continued healing.

Unfortunately, it wasn't long before we learned that our period of jubilance would be short-lived. Toward the end of the trip, she became fatigued and accidentally bit her tongue. Not only did the wound not heal, but it led to the discovery of a very painful and debilitating oral cancer. Over the next several weeks, this powerful woman of God drew even closer to the Lord, while her body experienced pain and weakness. It became so bad that our pastor's heart heeded the call to remain at home with her and leave the preaching to a few guest speakers who graciously stepped in to fill the void. One of them was his oldest son, Cam. This young, Word-infused pastor delivered weekly sanctuary and online messages that not only honored our Heavenly Father, but also brought doses of wholesome pride to his tender parents who needed the type of medicine that only God can provide. And then it hit me...he wasn't just a guest speaker; he was a prototype of the 11-year-old boy mentioned earlier who stepped in and completed the roofing project when his dad had to leave abruptly. What made it even more amazing is that he had to shoulder the responsibility of preaching to many people while his heart was breaking at the thought of his mom's physical suffering.

All the while, his dad's emotional pain weighed heavier as the days and nights slowly passed. It gets even "better." Often, the younger son or daughter (Carson and Kelsey) would sit with mom and hold her hand while tuning in to watch the church service online during those occasions when Pastor Kelvin would come in to preach a sermon. This was family at its best; a family whose strength came from our awesome God Who installed—and instilled—the principles of fatherhood into an earthly son (Kelvin's dad), who then passed them on to **his** son (Pastor Kelvin), then down to **his** son (Pastor Cam), who by example is now showing his own elementary-aged son what an honorable dad looks like.

The tossing of the car keys from a trusting dad to his son is a true account that the Poughkeepsie pastor shared at the men's conference on that Friday evening many years ago. Moreover, it symbolizes the kind of fatherly faith that can have lasting effects on the growth and development that a son desperately needs along life's journey. Calcium is good for building strong bones, but the trust and love of a father is great for building character. It has always been...and it will be that way...always.

Many generations have come and gone since then, but they have lost their ability and/or desire to pass this treasure along to their sons. With that, it has become more difficult for dads of dedication and nobility to avoid extinction. Don't **you** be among those who perpetuate the myth that good fathers are few and far between. Unless your son feels secure in the love you have poured into him, he is being sent off into a wildfire of challenges, unequipped to face the struggles of being a man of good reputation. He needs you in the beginning, at the end, and during all points in between. Without you, his journey is likely to be brutal and fruitless, and may very well cause damage to him and all who follow behind.

2

Home "Bittersweet" Home

F inding the most accurate beginning to this saga is sort of easy. Rehashing it is not. Yet, it's an essential component to use while closing an old chapter and opening a new one. Ask me where I left my eyeglasses, parked the car a few hours ago, or what I ate for breakfast yesterday, and I'll need a minute to think about it. But with very little effort I can clearly recall how fascinated I was with my grandfather's violin when I was three years old. Unfortunately, he would pass away not long afterward, so he never got to teach me how to play it.

When I turned five, my senses were a work in progress, so I relied on my sister's instincts to guide me. Denise's being older by 1 ½ years made it appear as though she had everything all figured out, even at her young age. With playtime, food, and TV in the mix, all seemed well enough. I mean, what more could we ask for? It turns out that it was soon to be a wide open-ended question which would require a lot of time to answer.

I can't say I remember dad being home much. We knew he lived there, and we'd see him occasionally. However, some of the things we witnessed were haunting, and left me confused and scared. Imagine this: We lived in a development named The Patterson Houses—a .k.a. "the projects"—in the South Bronx of New York City. The buildings were close and so were the apartments, which meant that what you weren't privy to firsthand, you heard about it later. One night, I was in the living room when my mom opened the door to let two neighbors in who were carrying our father. He was extreme-ly intoxicated and bleeding. The rest was a blur, so I couldn't tell you exactly where they placed him or how my mother handled the whole situation. All I know is that it was not a pretty sight, and I was devastated. That was probably my earliest recollection of being embarrassed.

I might be mistaken, but I believe that there was more than one instance when a couple of the neighborhood men had to help him home. Other times, he didn't come home at all. Those occasions grew more frequent as the weeks and months passed. I couldn't tell if my sister was feeling the same way I was because she had a knack for keeping her emotions concealed. However, mom was noticeably upset by this continuing saga. While I was lying in bed one summer evening, I heard her crying in the next room. By then I was about nine, and old enough to understand that this was **not** the way family life was supposed to be. My prayer that night was not for God to "lay me down to sleep." Rather, it was to help me to become a good man, and to honor my promise to be a great husband and father. It was the first time I had ever made an oath to the One I knew as God. I didn't know His name or where He lived, but I truly believed in Him and wanted Him to know that I had been paying attention and that I would not follow the example that was being played out before me.

Time passed by slowly. By then, dad was not living at home anymore. Well, that's not altogether true. In time we learned that he had taken up with another woman and moved in with her and her family. The irony of it all is that he lived on a street named "Home Street." (The jokes write themselves.) I knew this because whenever Father's Day came around, my mom would have my sister and me mail a card to him at that address. That was a sign that he wasn't coming back, so I accepted it painfully and somehow managed to become accustomed to him not being around. At least, for the time being. I would come to realize later that I never fully adjusted to his absence. There were moments when I'd be cruising along, thinking that everything was great, and other times when I'd sink into a depression even when I was too young to understand why.

*****Dads: Note to self...your children will*
***NEVER** get over it!!!*

Benched

Our apartment building stood 13 stories tall at the base of a cul-de-sac. A few yards away and adjacent to the entrance was an L-shaped bench. That bench faced 3rd Avenue, which was the main road up the block. Concrete supports and sturdy wooden slats made it perfect to be used as a base for games my friends and I would play, initials we'd carve, and portable record players to rest on while vinyl music filled the air with the *"Motown Sound."* It was on that bench that I would find myself deep in thought about the *Whys* and *Hows* of youngster life. I'd look up at the sky and watch airplanes passing overhead while wondering what held them up. The law of gravity was very new to me, but the "law" of **deprivation** was a concept that was rapidly becoming an unwanted companion the longer I sat there.

Cars coming down the street toward me and then turning at the bend in the road were also an attraction. Much time and effort went into trying to understand the mechanics behind how they worked. From airplanes to cars, I enjoyed watching them, but my focus was on buses. Not all buses, just the #26 Eastchester Road bus. That's the one my dad should have been riding on during the days when he promised to come and pick me up so I could spend time with him. Oddly enough, while I was waiting for him, I don't remember anyone else sitting near me. It's as if an invisible *"Do not Disturb"* sign was posted for the purpose of maintaining my privacy. That was okay for then, but for now in this retrospective moment, I invite all absent fathers to have a seat next to me and allow your imagination to record this scenario:

From where I sat, the 3rd Avenue traffic traveled north to south about a city block in distance up the street. Once it crossed my view, it disappeared behind a couple of the tall project buildings before pulling up to the bus stop which can only be seen after getting up from the bench and running into the clearing. One after another, passengers would get off, and dad would be nowhere in sight. The doors closed, the bus pulled away, and I'd return to the bench and wait another 20 minutes for the next #26 bus to come along. In-between that time the anxiety would build again, and the painful sequence repeated until dusk turned the passengers into silhouettes. Finally, I'd go home feeling rejected without being old enough to comprehend fully what I was experiencing. All I knew was that this weird, gut-wrenching sensation lasted until I slept it off. Sleeping it off was one thing...that feeling **wearing** off was another.

I even remember that there were back-to-back years when he promised to come and take my sister and me to get a Christmas tree. Same expectations, same outcome. As always, mom played the role of hero and saved the day. She would take us through the cold night air to get that tree. We'd drag it home, decorate it, and wake to see it overflowing with presents on Christmas morning. Sometimes we were "fortunate" to hear from dad by phone days later, but his brief conversations were incoherent, unapologetic, and without substance. Strangely, over time, the frequent letdowns did not have the same effect on me as they once did. Mom was beginning to look more like the mentor, although at a young age I had a feeling that she was playing a dual role. She taught me to tie my shoelaces and a necktie when I got a little older, as well as gentlemanly things such as taking off my hat when entering someone's house and waiting for them to offer me a seat before sitting down. Those were basics, but I would notice later on that she struggled with manly things. Still, she was awesome at juggling responsibilities.

Model Trains...Models Train

Saturday morning cartoons with waffles, roller skates, and stick ball games in the big park; these were a few of my favorite things. (No, I'm not gonna sing.) Then came Sunday newspaper funnies and bakery goods, followed by triple-header features at the local movie theater. These were all abundant joys that kept me going! Ahh yes...the good old weekends during the 50's and 60's! That's right, I'm dating myself now with no "Smitties" (pride) holding me back. Besides, this period will bear a greater significance as we proceed. Superheroes arose and action figures were right behind them: Batman; GI Joe; Superman and more. Surprisingly, mom was not included among them, but she sure enough should have been! I didn't fully appreciate her then, but looking back has me seeing her as an extended definition of a *palindrome*. More than just a word that spells the same forward and backward, mom was truly the same going and coming. Her consistency in caring and sacrificing for her children is worthy of never-ending thanks and praise. Interestingly, the word *dad* is also a palindrome, but unfortunately in this case it seems to have been one-directional only.

> ****This is a good time to mention that this book is NOT about bashing or bitterness. It is about forgiveness, healing, and recognition. It is also intended to be an encouragement for fathers (young and old), as well as single moms who are bearing the burden of raising children alone.* ***

One Christmas, mom bought me a .027-gauge Lionel Train Set and I was on cloud nine! She showed me how to interlock the tracks, connect the cars, respect the electricity, and use the transformer to make the train move. I had seen the pictures of little boys wearing the over-sized engineer's cap with the smiling dad beside them while they operated the set, but that scene was surely not an enactment in my household. It was my mother who was becoming my "locomotive" …my driving force. She was the engineer who would encourage me to broaden my scope and not sink into a bench of unmet expectations. She taught me—as best she could—how to use empathy, creativity, and sensitivity to build the type of character that would develop a godly stature and bring nobility to my future family. Sometimes the ride was smooth, other times it was a bit shaky. I was still moving in the right direction because **she** was the "train" model set before me.

It appears that mothers are born with an extra something. Don't they remember (or even understand) what the Lord meant when He said, "I will greatly multiply your sorrow and your conception; In pain you shall bring forth children?" Genesis 3:16 (NKJV)

Sounds like rough goings from the moment she conceives, and during the actual delivery of her baby. What's more, there's a good chance she will experience many painful moments throughout her lifetime as she weans, nurtures, protects, and sends her children off to find their place and purpose in a world that is nowhere near as gentle as she is.

With all of that on her, it's no secret that she was **never** meant to have to do it alone. She is configured to be the organizer and adhesion of the home. Much like the conductor of a train, her job is to oversee the well-being of others (in her case, children and husband) and secure the compartments for safe traveling. Just how is she supposed to do all of that, then run to the front of the train and be the engineer too? Yet, our mom did it, and single moms are still doing it to this day.

The mysteries of motherhood are mind-boggling. It is laced with indescribable strengths along with never-ending moments of those soft words and deeds that, sooner or later, leave her children amazed and feeling incredibly blessed. Her touch soothes, corrects, assures, supports, and always finds a way to remind you that your bond is as special as it gets. She is always there with you and there **for** you.

A mom's role is stretched to an often-unbearable limit without a father to solidify the family with his unique brand of love and protection. Our home was sweet because mom made it that way. However, a bitter vapor loomed since the absence of dad made it lack completeness. At that early stage of my life, it was hard for me to give up on the hope that he would come back. He **must** come back! I **needed** him to come back! Without him I'd feel lost and unwanted. Hanging on that dream, I'd wait.

Enter, Mr. Rob. He was a neighbor in our building who was married with three daughters. From my bench and beyond, I'd witness his goings and comings. Mr. Rob was a friendly, upright young husband and dad with a short height but a very tall presence. He had neighborly love and integrity written all over him. This man didn't demand respect, he attracted it! Often his car would be parked in an area where known "mischievous" characters were in abundance, but everyone knew him and knew his car as well. He'd walk through the gauntlet of drug transactions and receive nothing but warm greetings before driving off to work. He was an awesome family man, and because of the way he carried himself, his wife and children were favored throughout the neighborhood. I watched and took mental notes. When he and his family moved away, there went my role model. That's okay, though; by then I saw all I needed to see!

I kept in touch with Mr. Rob and called him every Father's Day. While proud to refer to him as "dad," he was equally as proud to call me "son." His whole family loved our exchange and even his daughters recognized me as the brother they never had. Years later, it was time to share my little secret with him. In a moment of sheer spontaneity, I wrote him a letter telling him how I used to watch him and adopted him as my role model. I explained how he was the example I needed, and that his integrity gave me a code to live by.

When he called me on the phone after reading the letter he was in tears. I was pretty choked up too as I explained how much of an impact he had on my life. What made my gesture even more special to him was that I expressed my admiration **before** he became stricken with cancer. His passing away months later was devastating. Still, he left a legacy with me that I will never forget!

Many of us have (or had at some point) a person we used as a standard to follow. We were watching them, mimicking them, wanting to be just like them. As a youngster, examining their character doesn't usually matter as much as what they did and how attractive they looked while doing it. All that's important is that they made a game-winning shot at the buzzer, won the gold medal at the Olympics, or signed a multi-million-dollar recording contract. During a few brief seasons working as a youth basketball referee, I was amazed to see some of these little guys wearing headbands, having mouth pieces hanging from their lips, and running up and down the court dribbling a ball that looked like it was much bigger than they could handle. They would even try to fuss in disbelief whenever a foul was called against them.

There is absolutely nothing wrong with striving to become a professional in any capacity, but wanting to be a celebrity for the fame and fortune with little (if any) concern about good character and integrity is not what a youngster should set as their main goal. "Daddy-coaches" should drill into them that practicing good sporting conduct is even more important than spending hours working on your craft or talent. One day those professional achievements will expire, while the curtain on the remnants of noble esteem will never come down.

Often, that inconspicuous role model is right before our eyes. It's that person who not only seems to do the right thing but is noticeably disappointed in themselves when they miss the mark. These are the ones who swim against the current of the cultural norms and commit to a lifestyle replete with honorable behaviors. What's special about this type of model is that he (or she) isn't concerned with who's watching, nor are they seeking high praise for good deeds or charming mannerisms. Theirs is an unassuming personality that captures the attention of a formidable soul who's observing, learning, and desirous of being just like that model when they grow up. You may think you're just going about with routine, everyday functions - but keep in mind...someone may be watching your every move and saying to themselves "**That's** who I want to be like!"

Again, thanks Mr. Rob!

When is the last time you used the word *scrumptious*? I did just other day and thought immediately, "Wow, where did I dig that up from?"

Let's face it, there is a plethora (oops...there I go again) of words we seldom use or never use at all. Okay, so how long has it been since you've hand-written a letter? Or rode a unicycle, went skydiving, or let a llama spray your face? I'll bet that for most of us, all of these are things that we rarely do or will never want to do.

How about agreeing to participate in a unique challenge instead? For one whole day, pretend that people are watching you as though you're their secret role model. This could range from friends, coworkers, or even total strangers. Your job is to be mindful of your every word and/or action that might leave them so impressed with how you conduct yourself, that they would see you as someone to emulate going forward. To bring this experiment into the theme of our context, be that man who considers the possibility that his spectator might be a boy or adolescent in desperate need of an admirable role model. Give it a try. No doubt, someone will be watching!

Next is the role model who is aware that he's one. This man is dedicated to being involved in hands-on training. He is deliberate in setting good examples and makes a conscious effort to have a positive impact on a youngster's formative years.   He plants the seeds, explains what kind of "fruit" will be produced, then, in time, he enjoys the budding of good growth revealed. As the two interact, life's lessons are addressed, and wise counsel is freely given.

Sometimes a young boy/man will learn by just observing how his mentor handles any given situation. Other times, verbal instructions create a better learning experience and the two might even volley ideas, which is a great way of making an apprentice feel as though his input is valuable. An awesome bonus is a God-fearing, Bible-based type of leader! That way, his examples will be coming from the highest standard possible.

In this instance it would surely seem appropriate to call on the Bible verse which reads, "Train up a child in the way he should go, and when he is old he will not depart from it." Proverbs 22:6 (NKJV)

However, it would be wise to examine that Scripture closer for a clear interpretation of its meaning since we all know of children who **were** trained properly and yet allowed their "folly" to lead them astray. It has been suggested that the true interpretation of the verse has to do with recognizing a child's talent and working with them to hone it. That way, when they're older it becomes an established career that will help support themselves and their family. Bear in mind I wouldn't be too quick to embrace that translation as dogmatic since some have turned away from their talents to seek questionable professions.

What Goes Around, Goes Around

"What goes around, comes around" is the expression we often use to describe the principle that a person will be treated the same way that they treat others. But what happens when the scenario begins with a person **being** mistreated? In this case, the child is the victim of an absent dad. They aren't the ones initiating the infraction, they're on the **receiving** end of it. It's already come around, and often because it came around from their dad's dad. Here is where it might get a little tricky. That boy is likely to grapple with feelings of rejection. Low self-esteem then ushers in an ongoing, laborious effort to be noticed (sometimes in the wrong way). As he gets older, he can become embittered for having to go through the process of growing up alone, all while constantly having to prove himself to be a real man without understanding what that really looks like. Unless he's determined to break the cycle, he might very well end up being the same absent or neglectful father that his dad was to him.

It wasn't until I was a young adult that my aunt (my dad's sister) told the tale of how their father walked away from the family. She didn't explain what happened, only that he was estranged and that she and her siblings had no interaction with him. Auntie went on to tell how she spotted her dad in a subway car one day when she was much older. After approaching him in a tender daddy-to-daughter manner, she said, "Hi daddy." He stiffened, continued reading his newspaper, and totally ignored her, reaffirming his position of a dad who had no place in his life for her or the family. She was crushed and found it impossible to contain her sorrow in front the surrounding onlookers! Her brothers (that would include my dad), she added, were just as devastated as if they were present when it happened.

This means that since they did not have a relationship with their dad—and mom's dad passed away when I was three years old—I never got to enjoy a grandfather-grandson bond either.

As broken as they all were, someone recently stated that only a broken man can walk away from his children. Perhaps **his** father had walked away from him! When an emotional funnel cloud starts swirling at ground zero, it develops into a raging tornado that destroys every-thing in its path. No doubt, my dad was demolished, and as a result, I was too.

I've spent a lifetime wondering if the Lord didn't allow me to have children of my own because in His omniscience, He thought I would perpetuate the pain, but I always dismiss that suspicion because it would go against the grain of my character. He and I both know that I couldn't do that to my children, especially after feeling the pain that it caused me.

On the flip side, there are some success stories out there! We read about a couple of them in the opening chapter of this book. Countless more men like those are undocumented, and sadly, worthy fathers don't get the credit or recognition they deserve. You are the true heroes of history, the giants in a land ripe with young boys aching for a dad to love and guide them. Your selfless leadership and sacrifice are worthy of the greatest respect possible that any person can receive. Instinctively, and without hesitation, you allow your son to view life from behind your back of protection.

At the proper time, you'll bring him up alongside you so that he can learn to keep in step with the rhythms of day-to-day involvements. Finally, there will be a grand moment when he is able to take the lead and be the trailblazer of his own family. If that includes a son (or sons), he (or they) will also have a template to follow. By the standards of today's society, it's hard to imagine it getting any better than this, but believe it or not, it can. If **any** dad comes to a point where he decides to use the Bible as his divine absolute, then he has entered the upper echelons of good fathering. He will have the best Instruction "Emanuel" (Manual) to follow **and** to guide him as he leads. His legacy continues in supreme fashion down the line, and the beat goes on!

3

Strike Three!

Through it all, that "waiting bench" became a symbol of unattained patience, hope, disappointment, and a place that screamed *Rejected!* It would not be long before I'd move on to another bench - a Little League baseball team bench. I'd sit on that one too. Waiting. This time, as an 11-year-old hoping that dad would come to see me play. Instead, I settled for witnessing the look of pride on other dads' faces when their sons got a hit or made a spectacular catch.

Thankfully, my mom managed to come to a game one day. She would have attended more often if her work schedule allowed. I was glad to see her, but it just wasn't the same. Somehow, I entered a strange zone. Without any great effort, I began to realize that my wish for dad to return home—or at best, to be with me on occasions—was nothing more than a pipe dream.

I remember sitting in the barbershop as a little New York Yankees fan a day or two after Roger Maris hit his season's record-setting 61st home run. The barbers and some customers couldn't stop talking about it and I was more than okay with that. Living not too far from the stadium was a treat - not only because I could attend some of the games, but many nights I was excited to hear the roar of the crowd from my bedroom window. My friends and I sat in those "expensive" 75-cent bleachers seats in the outfield right behind a couple of famous Yankees: #7 (Mickey Mantle), and #9 (Roger Maris). We had even more fun going to the games on days that were designated as Bat

Day or Ball Day. That was when all fans would receive a bat or ball as a souvenir when going through the ticket gate.

If they only knew how I longed for a **_Dad Day_**. Imagine receiving one of **those** as a souvenir!

Anyway, as a young baseball enthusiast, wanting to grow up to be a professional player was a constant fantasy. I had most of the baseball cards and chewed all the bubble gum that came with them. I even fanned the deck at times to select a player randomly that I'd pretend to be before I played some of the games on the neighborhood playground. Since the Yankees' catcher (Elston Howard) looked a lot like me, I often picked his card and focused on honing my skills in that position behind the plate. I became pretty good at it although I didn't have the brawn that most catchers had back then.

Another interesting baseball personality was an umpire named Emmett Ashford. He was Major League Baseball's first umpire of color and was most colorful in nature as well. His animated style of trotting down the foul line between innings provided the crowd with a unique showmanship that was very entertaining although his career was launched during a time when racial discrimination was just as prevalent on the diamond as it was everywhere else. Regardless, his skin was as thick as it was dark, and he overcame the occasional mistreatment he encountered. His style and stature might have even been a subliminal implant that would later entice me to become an umpire years later.

Allow me to fast-forward to that experience before bringing us back to the present.

***

Becoming a baseball umpire was never in my plans. Toward the end of my competitive softball career as a middle-aged adult, I was offered the opportunity to officiate games within the same league where I played. It was okay, but I still didn't see it as a role that I would perform for long. When a few certified Amateur Softball Association (A.S.A.) umpires spotted me working some games, they invited me to join their ranks. Since they also officiated Little League baseball games, I trained for that too and became more involved with that sport. From there, I joined a different association whose umpires worked scholastic games, moving me up to Junior Varsity and ultimately High School Varsity games.

As the years passed, I started officiating college level games and went on to adult baseball leagues. Looking back on my career as an umpire after 19 years, the one thing each level of players and their fans had in common all too often was poor sporting conduct. Gone were the days when it was a game of having fun. The game has now become an obsession with winning and insulting officials, and an overall inability to recognize that there are much more serious matters in life than coming out on top in every contest. Regardless of how that may sound, I've had more pleasant encounters than unpleasant ones. I took advantage of many opportunities to coach youngsters who misbehaved or put themselves down during or after a not-so-good performance on the field. I exhorted many of them over the years to cherish having their dads loving them enough to attend their games and even practice with them to help them get better. On the flip side, I've also reminded lots of dads who put heavy demands on their sons that they should feel blessed to have children because some of us weren't as fortunate in that regard. Looking back, I believe it was God's way of spoon-feeding me the notion that my calling had less to do with baseball and fatherhood, and more to do with me allowing Him to use me to edify others. After a long stint, it was **_Ball Four_**, and time for me to **_Walk_**.

Thanks for letting me digress. Now, back to the past.

***

I was heading into adolescence, and my focus was on baseball, friends, and fun. With that, I managed to convince myself that I was fine without a dad. Little did I know that my plight was just beginning and a lifelong trek through very rough (yet, inconspicuous) emotional terrain was waiting for me.

Although time often appeared to be standing still, suddenly I was a 10th grade high school student. My overall grades weren't too bad, but neither was I honor roll material. I was just coasting along, waiting for the final senior bell to ring in a couple of years so I could get on with my life. Baseball became my obsession, and I was growing in my talent. My dream was to be a major league player (as was the case with many guys my age). My grand moment came when I tried out for—and made—my school's varsity team! As a sophomore, that was like making it to the pros! The coach explained to me that I was a bit undersized for a catcher, which I already knew, but he liked my skills. He went on to say that I wouldn't see much action my first season because it would be more of an observing and learning experience. *No problem*, I thought. I was just so proud to make the team!

The next week I showed up for an indoor practice in the gym which was also a special session for straggler pitchers who missed tryouts. In my eagerness to fit in, I asked the coach if he wanted me to warm up one of them. He said, "Sure."

During those days a catcher wasn't required to wear a protective mask while warming up a pitcher when there was no batter in the box, but after catching a few throws from him I wished I had worn one. That ball came zipping in with a velocity that made me uncomfortable. As if that wasn't enough, it appeared to be a fastball with a weird break to it just before popping my mitt. I gotta admit, I felt a little out of my league and started getting nervously distracted. The next pitch came in and all I remember was the blow to my face and lying on the gym floor with a bloody mouth while a small crowd of players stood over me. The coach helped me up and wasted no time saying, "I think you need to come back next year when you get a little bigger."

As if being bloody, in great pain, and embarrassed wasn't enough, I now had to deal with another BIG dose of rejection!

My trip home was a long one because I commuted to that school. I had to ride the subway with people staring at my blood-soaked, battered face. Holding that handkerchief against my mouth was one thing, holding in the tears was another.

When I finally arrived at home, I lost it! Mom tried her best to console me, and even encouraged me to try out for the junior varsity team, but I was in too much physical and emotional pain to appreciate her efforts. I knew what—or rather, who—I needed.

****Dads out there, have those "Get back up on the horse" speeches ready for them! Moms are equipped with an instinctive way of caressing and soothing those sensitive sore spots, but it's YOUR paternal bandage that helps not only heal the wound, but it also replenishes a son's and/or daughter's confidence.*

A couple of weeks passed before tryouts for the JV squad was held. By then I had somewhat recovered from my setback and reluctantly showed up for it, but when I walked into the gym, that same pitcher with the blazing fastball was there also attempting to make the squad. No way was I going to allow myself to be paired up with that guy again, so I turned and walked out without even breaking stride. Thus, my baseball "career" ended before it even began.

Meanwhile, I drifted without plan or purpose. Baseball had been my passion and the only interest that kept me excited. Without it, I was a mid-teenager with idle time on my hands and too much homework! Since my detachment from the sport that I had devoted myself to for several years had happened so abruptly, the reality that a new pastime had to replace it wasn't ever a thought. Academics? Not a viable candidate. Something else would surely take its place eventually. No hope. No courage. No educational motivation. I struck out during my last at bat and headed for the "locker room."

Feeling rejected wasn't foreign to me, but by now I was feeling **dejected** on top of that.

Fuzzy Feelings

The clock and calendar were working in unison to mess with my head. One minute it seemed as if time was at a standstill, while at other times it felt like it was hurrying me into a place for which I was unprepared. I began ignoring serious matters and laughing at cartoons. Next, I'd switch gears and start laughing at serious matters while beginning to analyze cartoons. I even spent quality time trying to figure out why Popeye and Bluto would go crazy over Olive Oyl whenever she came on the scene.

I mean, hadn't they heard of Betty Boop? What would they do if **she** stepped into the frame? Am I missing something here? The girl in my Science class is cute, but so is the one down the street in one of the other apartment buildings. Mom and sister are more like roommates at this point, and it seemed as though they were making nothing more than cameo appearances in my sphere of developments. Soon it seemed as though I was standing behind Rod Serling on the TV show "The Twilight Zone" as he said, "Submitted for your approval."

Things were changing in and around me, and I didn't understand why. All I knew was that a piece of scab under my chin was stubbornly hanging on while I constantly tried to pick it off. I plucked at it for a few days before finally looking in the mirror to see why it wouldn't budge. And there it was! It wasn't a scab at all, it was a single hair waiting for the rest of the fuzz to grow in around it. I was getting a beard! The shadow of a mustache snuck up on me also. It was a cavalcade of hormones invading my being and forcing me into maturity. I'd heard of these chemical messengers but I was ignorant as to what they were and how I was to respond to them. There were other strange sensations in the mix also, so I knew it was time to have a conversation with somebody. But who? Can't go to mom with this because it was clearly a male issue. Besides, our relationship had taken a turn by then and we weren't in synch much anymore.

Obviously, there was no dad to go to for explanations. No grandfather, big brother, or uncle either. I thought about approaching Mr. Rob, but he worked a lot and was busy with his own family. I'd just have to figure this all out by myself.

So often this is the case with many young fellows. They're left to struggle with ambiguities and often turn to inappropriate resources for aid. Since a young mind is still under construction and can't always discern the difference between good advice and bad advice, there are always risk factors that can contribute to confusion and sometimes even cause damaging consequences depending on the importance of the decision. Let's just add that to the growing list of why the need for a father's input and directives prove to be vital during the adolescent phase. Up to this point, life used to be so easy.

Choices were made for me, but suddenly, I had to start making some choices on my own.

It's funny how retrospect has a way of turning out to be a great tutor. I don't remember where I learned it, but as a teenager I thought I had rights and was entitled to exercise them. Even funnier is how many of those rights ended up being wrongs! If I had only realized that although I was given a free will to make choices, demanding my rights as an unfledged mini man with a single chin hair was a reckless move. As *The Doobie Brothers* would say, "What a Fool Believes!"

It would be much further along before I finally understood that regardless of how aged and experienced a person becomes, they still can fall victim to this kind of thinking.

Remember as little kids how we'd sometimes keep turning ourselves around and around until dizziness came over us? Wasn't that fun? I mean, dumb? The room was spinning out of control and we'd just laugh ourselves into a frenzy. Nowadays it's called Vertigo and instead of laughing, we vomit! Well, my life was somewhat like that experience during this period. I wasn't sure which theories and opinions to believe. Moreover, my own identity hadn't completely formed, and true meanings were still being deliberated. I was in dire need of recognition and affirmation. If things didn't change soon, who knows where I'd end up. Santa Claus wasn't real to me anymore, but that Boogie Man was still hanging out and scaring me into believing that bad times were waiting for me just ahead.

My perception of the world around me was no longer that of a place flowing with milk and honey. President Kennedy had been assassinated, super-power nations were threatening to annihilate each other, and discrimination was running rampant. *The Supremes* had every right to ask, "Where Did Our Love Go?" and *The Temptations* nailed it with "Ball of Confusion!" Oh yes, the "Lazy, Hazy, Crazy Days of Summer" *(Nat King Cole)* were upon us, but it wasn't because of

"Soda, and Pretzels, and Beer." It was because society had stepped on a banana peel and all handrails had been removed! Smiles weren't as pronounced. Manners weren't as instinctive - and no one seemed to care that I was "Stuck in the Middle" *(Stealers Wheel)* of this madness with disobedient hormones! I did my best to stop myself from "Going in Circles," but *The Friends of Distinction* were no help at all!

Yes, I do believe that music did (and always will) soothe the savage beast and it did help ease my mind a little, but my mission became even more pronounced. I still had to make it through high school— "Alone again, Naturally"— *(Gilbert O'Sullivan)*. C'mon man, you can do this. I'm gonna take that "Long and Winding Road" *The Beatles* sang about, and find my way.

Meanwhile, I had two more years of *Ache-ademics*.

Ugh!

4

Off to "Sea" Things Differently

My junior year in high school was disastrous! Without having formal conversations about birds, bees, or hormones, my idea of important things started to take on a distorted view. How could my superhero mom suddenly morph from a loving parent wisely instructing me, into someone who was now bossing me around? (I didn't realize it at the time, but **I** was the one changing, not her). Rebellion set in, playing hooky from school followed, and before long, I didn't care about much of anything.

Miraculously, I was promoted to the 12th grade, but instead of having plans in place for college, I found myself playing catch-up since I didn't have enough credits to graduate with my senior classmates. My option? Work all summer, return to school in the fall as a "super senior" and graduate in January. Through that same distorted lens, I saw myself as a failure and a person desperately in need of a plan to feed some purpose and pride into an empty soul. I absolutely MUST do something to build self-esteem that had no foundation or structure. It's now or never!

The wheels in my brain were turning and so were the ones on my bicycle that hot summer afternoon in August of 1969. I rode to a Recruiting Station quite a distance from where I lived and circled the building a few times before nervously going inside. When I did go in, that Marine Corp Recruiter arose from his seat like I was a commanding officer popping in for a surprise inspection. His was a crafty sale and in a flash, I had papers, handshakes, and a promise that my enlistment would be almost as good as sitting under a palm tree on a tropical island. My official swearing-in was scheduled for two weeks later.

Wow…what just happened here?

Part of me felt pretty good about making the first major decision on my own. On the other hand, this was during the height of the Vietnam War, which meant that the "palm tree" was probably going to be more like a camouflaged bush. That's okay. After all, this was, *"The Few. The Proud. The Marines."* - and I needed a quick dose of pride and courage to help develop my manhood.

Committing to serve in the U.S Marine Corp was a cakewalk compared to announcing the news to my mother. She was devastated. Not many words were exchanged, but just as I had overheard her crying in her bedroom about nine years prior, history repeated itself. This time, though, I clearly heard her saying to someone on the phone—in a sobbing, shaken voice— "I think he's doing this because of me."

Although we were more at odds with each other during that period, it bothered me that she was heartbroken over my plan. So, after being convinced by a friend's older brother who was serving in the Navy, and another friend's dad who had previously served in that branch as well, I went back to the recruiting station and switched from the "Proud" to the "Persuaded." You see, back then (and perhaps it's still the same today) although signing papers agreeing to enlist in a branch of the military was huge, it was not a done deal until you were officially sworn in. How did the Marine Recruiter take the news that I wanted to change over? Well, let's just say he was hotter than the jungles of Vietnam, and twice as offensive!

I beat the early birds when I got out of bed on that cool, cloudy, quiet morning of August 27th, 1969. In all honesty, I didn't really sleep much the night before, knowing that my life was about to change forever. My friend, Joe, kept me company into the wee hours of the morning. We reminisced about good times, and he left me with enough time to be able to grab a few hours of sleep before daybreak. After giving my mother and sister a hug, I walked away slowly from the apartment building that had been home for the past 18 years. Looking back one last time, I saw mom waving to me from the hallway window until I turned the corner as she disappeared from my view. I boarded a subway train to downtown New York City and reported to the processing center to be sworn in and transported to the Naval Boot Camp in Great Lakes, Illinois. No turning back now. I was property of The U.S. Navy, and my new "parents" were a bunch of seemingly disgruntled uniformed men yelling commands at me from a proximity without any regard for social distancing!

What in the world have I gotten myself into?

Ironically, my cartoon hero was Popeye. But unfortunately, I was way past the age of believing that a can of spinach was going to help get me out of this situation. I had to tough it out, which was why I was there in the first place...to tough it out! Once I figured out that this was truly my action plan being carried out, I not only adapted, but I went on to advance to the highest rank possible during my enlistment. First things first.

Three months of recruit training was intense and stretched us to mental and physical extremes that we didn't think was possible. When it was over, I was an inch closer to the man I had set out to be, but there was much more ground to cover before my mission would be fully accomplished. The real action was waiting for me across thousands of miles of water in the form of a Naval Destroyer aptly named the U.S.S Strong. How's that for aligning with my plan to toughen up? The ship was only a couple of weeks into a six-month deployment overseas, so it would be a little while before I'd catch up with my crew. My orders were official, and things were about to get very interesting.

But first I was headed home on a two-week leave to see my mom, sister, and friends.

Be it Ever so Humble...

...there is no place like home! Being away for three months seemed more like three years. I was greeted by all the above with tight hugs and warm welcomes. You'd think I just performed a heroic act or something. I loved it! Do I dare even think about how awesome it would be if dad was there? Oh well, focus, man...stay the course!

"Can't hang too long, guys, I'm shipping out just before Christmas ("The First Noel" away from home and so far away)."

The end of my stay came quickly, and the heaviness was unbearable when it was time to leave. There were a few stopovers which included transients in Philadelphia, PA; Rota, Spain; and Germany, where I was transported via a WWII cargo plane to Athens, Greece. Finally, I met up with the "Strong." I would learn later that we even had a theme song titled "Only the Strong Survive" which would play over the PA system during key moments of our deployment. When I arrived at the pier where the ship was moored, it was dark, late, and two days before Christmas. Once again, I was feeling homesick.

The Reality of Fear

T-Bone steaks seem a lot less tasty when they're grilled on the fantail of a U.S. Destroyer while sailing through the Black Sea. That's an area the Russians claim as their territory. It's kind of hard to enjoy a barbeque with one eye on your plate and the other on an infestation of Soviet warships and a reconnaissance plane tracking us. However, it became traditional to flex our might by showing valor in adversarial waters. After all, how would it look if the U.S.S. Strong and a sister Destroyer hesitated to boldly make our presence known to our super-power counterparts? Still, that was always the dreaded part of our six-month deployments. Dangerous and tense situations were not frequent, but every now and then I was reminded that precision and extreme carefulness was my greatest protector. Or so I thought.

One night a terrible accident occurred. Our fleet was engaged in routine maneuvers when a Navy pilot from one of our aircraft carriers missed his landing and plunged his jet into the ocean. An extensive search for him was underway by all ships in the fleet, but it wasn't until the next morning that his body was recovered by our ship. Such a sad and sobering day.

My own close calls were acutely distressing as well. There were a couple of occasions when I was nearly washed overboard. Once while we were refueling, and another during a careless move on my part that's difficult to explain. It would later come to pass that I'd be stationed aboard an ammunition replenishment ship. That "home" was more like a floating time-bomb! Sometimes fire alarms—which turned out to be false—would go off, sending damage controllers running and searching for a potential fire in the magazines containing missiles. Those were some bone-chilling episodes that can haunt for a lifetime! Very scary indeed, but the most harrowing experience is as fresh in my mind as if it happened yesterday.

It's late-night February and our ship was in the remote parts of the Mediterranean Sea. I stepped out on deck with my back to the sea, knowing that it was pitch black outside, but I was still unprepared for what I was about to see. When I turned around there was a gigantic, deep orange-red orb sitting on the horizon. I froze in a motionless stance with my heart pounding in my chest while staring at the object convinced that it was an alien spaceship sitting on the water. I was certain that at any moment its mother ship would signal it to suck us in and carry us into space. I'm not sure how much time lapsed before the more reasonable part of my faculties kicked in and I realized that it was a harvest moon. But please don't think it's the same kind you come across suddenly while driving down the road in the evening. Rather, consider these enhancements: nighttime at sea has no street lamps, building lights, or any other optical obstructions to distract from the dark "curtain" around you. It's just a densely dark backdrop when it's cloudy, and a sparkling dark one on a clear night.

What the illusion does is magnify the objects in your vision. That means a harvest moon which is 238,900 miles away appears to be only as distant as the length of a football field! To fully engage your imagination, allow me to explain further.

I was brought on board ship as a sailor under the rate (or job title) of an Interior Communications Electrician. However, whenever a new sailor reports for duty, working within your job description is put on a 2-month delay until you finish what's called "mess duty." What that means is you must be an aid to the cooks in the galley as they prepare meals for the crew. At night they're working on breakfast for the next day. Your job is to do their grunt work, which includes dumping trash off the fantail (the very back of the ship) and into the ocean. Our galley was located near the front of the ship, so you'd have to walk your trash all the way to the rear and then walk back. With all that context laid out, let's get back to this new sailor standing awestruck with legs that were paralyzed with fear. Oh, I knew it was "just" the moon, but I perceived it as being more than that. I saw it as a huge, circular mass suspended in space by the power of God's design.

Likewise, so is the earth. Again, I was struck with reverential fear in that moment and couldn't move my legs. I somehow managed to move my arms, though, and throw the trash overboard from the very spot I was standing in, then I darted back inside the ship.

Describing something so amazing from 54 years ago clearly indicates how much of an impact it had on my mind that night. On the other hand, impacting my **heart** would require several more wakeup calls over a period of about 15 years. It's not that I was such a hard nut to crack, but more like a bruised young man who was an emotional nomad searching for love and affirmation from his father, and a means to qualify as a certified man.

Oh, if only I had keen foresight back then, I would have known that God's mission had dominion over my own. He had me sailing in waters and stepping onto land that is rich in biblical history. Some of those places I had seen pictures of but never knew the depths of their meanings were much greater than the oceans and seas I passed over. Little did I know as some shipmates and I rented motor scooters and rode around on the island of Crete (Greece's largest island) that the Apostle Paul visited that area on his way to Rome. It is also said to have been where Titus had his ministry. I toured places like the Acropolis, which was a fortress dating back to sometime around the 13th century B.C.E. and later became a religious center. It was among several of the Greek ruins I visited. While our ship was docked in Naples (Italy), I was fortunate to be able to tour and photograph some historical sites in Rome including the Catacombs and the Coliseum. All the while, I had no clue how meaningful those places were. I was out to find the "man" in me, while God's plan was for the man in me to find Him.

Occasional storms made it necessary for us to strap ourselves to our racks (bunks) in order to prevent us from rolling out; and eating with one hand while holding onto our trays with the other kept our food from ending up on the floor. One cloudy, stormy Thanksgiving I ventured topside just to have a little quiet time and think about home. It's funny how the greater the distance away you are from home, the more surreal the place seems to be. Were my teenage friends still hanging out at "Raymond's," playing records on the jukebox and having sodas?

It was like home didn't exist anymore. My better senses told me that it did, but it was still hard to believe. On the positive side, the further away I sailed, the closer I got to mom. No doubt, I was starting to really appreciate her love and guidance—which was probably a great first step toward maturity. It's strange how private times can sometimes have a way of pushing distractions to the side while you assemble life's jigsaw puzzle.

Since the Navy managed to play an important role in teaching me discipline and organizational skills, I advanced to the rank of 2nd Class Petty Officer and started to feel a morsel of pride budding within me. Yet, there was much more that I needed, because the effects of growing up in a household with an absent dad was unwilling to loosen its stubborn grip. Feelings of insufficiency rode me often, and had me asking the question, "Where does my life fit into God's grand scheme of things?"

But one special day I got the treat of my life. While walking through an airport on my way home for a two-week leave, I was in uniform and carrying my sea bag on my shoulder. As I passed a little boy and his mother, I overheard him say, "Look, mom, a real live sailor!" He was so excited, but little did he know that inside I was even more thrilled than he was! His words were such a boost to my undernourished ego! It was a temporal moment that I wished could have lasted much longer, especially since there was more egregious turbulence in my forecast. Still—for now—I took that small surge of endorphins and ran with it!

That "We may just be onto something here" way of thinking came over me as I began to see the Navy as a foundation for building my esteem. After all, they were doing a pretty good job of teaching me discipline, order, and teamwork, beginning with those bootcamp days of basic training. Marching in perfect unison with a large battalion has a way of instilling precision as a necessary component useful for the importance of unity. No, the Navy can't take full credit for that since it was originally God's idea for mankind, but the constant emphasis on it supported His divine concept. There is nothing like the beat of 80 pairs of boots in a synchronized cadence to act as a constant reminder of how effectively a unit can perform when all parts work together. That type of concentration and exactness is not just rhythmic, but it's the kind of oneness that can be a tool for learning how to function in any relationship in every walk of life.

What better place to prepare for those future connections than right there at home "marching" with dad while keeping stride with his steps as he teaches his son how to grow into a man? We may not end up walking in his exact footsteps, but the prints he lays out as a man of integrity will leave an indelible impression in the paths that are wise for us to follow.

> ***Dads, cherish those determinative years. Catch those young, wide, inquisitive eyes and submissive attitudes while in their early stages because they are extremely absorbent. Also, please don't think for one moment that young daughters are less deserving of your time and attention than your sons. Although the instructions from mom are more beneficial to them in terms of their transitioning into "ladyhood," they still notice qualities in you that help them to know what to look for when the courters come around.*

When I came to the end of my enlistment, civilian life met me at the gate. I felt confident that I'd slide right into a lucrative career since I had a technical trade to offer. Smoother sailing (on dry land) is certain to be my reward for having to endure the agitated currents of occasionally unfriendly oceans. The harsh reality was that that was then, and this is now. The clamor of loud, tempting voices increased in volume while God's still, small whispers were unintentionally muted by my selfishness and defiance. It was time to bring this "new and improved" guy back into the fray and show the world who I was now.

5

Smoke Gets in Your Eyes...

A nd when it does, it's painful. The irritation causes the eyes to get teary, red, and dry. It's interesting how these physical symptoms are interchangeable with emotional ones as well. What your eyes see—or don't see—can result in things becoming distorted and/or damaged, while perceptions are skewed, and many things often take on unrealistic attributes. In the physical eye, the cornea is the "windshield" that gets the direct hit from smoke in the environment. In addition to directing light into the eye, it acts as a protector of the Iris, Pupil, and Lens.

> *"The eye contains over two million working parts and is considered the second most complex organ in the body—the most complex is the brain."*[1]
> Dr. Russel Lazarus, Optometrist

The performance of these parts, then, is no doubt crucial to the overall functionality of the eye. Without them doing their part or when operating inefficiently, visual impairment will occur and will render it unable to see things as they should be seen. While examining how harmful smoke can be to the eyes and other parts of the body, it is just as important to understand how its effects can penetrate our soul also. I can certainly attest to that.

I was never a cigarette smoker. While not even being old enough to spell the word "cough," my first (and last) meeting with a "loosie" was in a secluded bathroom where I struck a match, struck a pose, and pretended to be a miniature version of a real man. It didn't go well at all. I almost choked to death and walked away wondering how anyone would want to condition themselves to enjoy doing that.

Regretfully, a short time after my honorable discharge from the Navy, I became a frequent marijuana smoker. The smoke was much milder so there were no choking episodes, and initially I found pleasure in the euphoric state I experienced as I smoked. What's more, I returned to my old neighborhood buddies who were now engaged in the same activity. I went from life on the high seas, to getting high on solid ground. I couldn't blame it on my dad. He wasn't around long enough for me to pick up the habit from him. Besides, his intoxicant of choice was alcohol, not marijuana. I was all in and nothing around me seemed to matter.

Hey Mom, I'm Home!

My years in the Navy were credited as military leave by the bank I had worked for before I enlisted, and they welcomed me back with open arms. So did mom, as I returned to live with her in the same apartment where I grew up. I enjoyed my job, the salary was good, and daily car-pooling with grass-smoking coworkers meant that I now had more friends who were participants in a routine that lured us into captivity. It became evident that some employees in the business district also indulged themselves in the same bad habit on a regular basis. Sometimes it was during lunch breaks, sometimes while commuting. (I am so ashamed to rehash this dark period of my life.)

Gradually, the atmosphere was starting to get a bit hazy from the use of a substance that was acting as a smokescreen by keeping us from seeing things as they truly were. By now the smoke was all around me. Everywhere I turned its vapors taunted me and took me to a place where it wasn't even enjoyable anymore. Instead, it had become nothing more than a routine. There were times when in-between tokes I still managed to ask myself, "What are you doing?" Not only that, but "**Why** are you doing this?"

I was too immature back then to answer that question, so I'd have to let my dilemma run its course. Next came the paranoia phase. Who's watching me? Is the redness of my eyes a dead giveaway? A couple of "get the redness out" drops would take care of that. Still, I wondered if it started to affect my speech or hinder my ability to hold a conversation. I think so, so let me just avoid people as much as I can. Nasal congestion was also a side effect of constant marijuana smoking. For that, I'd whip out my nasal inhaler and open my passage back up. I had it all figured out! Or so I thought.

My "308 buddies" would often wait for me to get home from work so that we could pile up in my car and joyride. One of our favorite things to do was to ride out of the projects and visit a liquor store far from the neighborhood where we would buy something in a brown bag to soothe our raspy throats caused by the excessive smoking and laughter. Humor was our trademark when we were in that state of exuberance. We would laugh at anything from a pigeon crossing the street, to a spit-bubble accidentally floating out of someone's mouth while speaking.

Not sure why the 9th cloud was the only one famous for epitomizing one's happiness, but we were there...until it happened. We were pulled over by a patrol car! I'm the driver, the car is packed to capacity with every eyeball as red as a traffic light, joints in our possession and throughout the vehicle, and the smell of marijuana permeating the compartment. We were reeking! I am amazed that the police officer didn't catch a buzz when I rolled down the window!

The deafening silence was broken when he said, "License, registration, and insurance card, please." We sat like choir boys as he took my information and went back to his patrol car. The minutes felt like days until he returned!

He handed me my documents and simply said, "You fellas be careful."

Wait a minute! No, "Step out of the vehicle," gathering up our paraphernalia, radioing for backup??? When the officer walked away, we were all in shock that not only weren't we issued a warning, but we were given what appeared to be a "blessing" instead! How could this be? I know, maybe that cop was preoccupied with his idea for a movie featuring a singing group called "The Five Heartbeats" which was inspired by five young men whose hearts were pounding through their chests after being pulled over for a routine traffic stop! The ride home was a noticeable contrast from the boisterous trip **to** the liquor store.

Too long ago to remember what we talked about, but I clearly recall what I **thought** about. I pondered the notion that perhaps sometimes God grants mercy to people even if they aren't in fellowship with Him. After all, here we were with the deck stacked against us and we were pardoned by a professional and polite officer of the law.

Whew...that was as close as it can get!

I decided that it was time to visit my dad. I had dropped by to see him a few times since coming home from the seas, but my stopovers were calculated and as brief as I could possibly make them. There were no hard feelings toward him, but Harry Chapin's *"Cats in the Cradle"* song lyrics summed it up best. With so many desolate years behind me, we sort of changed places. His life slowed down while mine got busy. Besides, he was still under the grip of alcohol which made for weightless and uncomfortable conversations. How's that for calling the kettle black? He drinks, I smoke "grass."

He was a mild-mannered man and funny at times without really trying to be, so sometimes my short-term visits were entertaining. But without the foundation of a father-son bond, my attention span was limited. Still, I'd drop by sporadically, especially since his (and his wife's) generosity was at its peak whenever they were in the cups.

So sad. Not only because of how his life declined into such a lethargic mode, but that I would exploit his condition by taking advantage of his oblivious charities. I knew it wasn't right, and I confess that I couldn't help feeling that he owed me for all the years that he was missing in action. I spent his "restitutions" recklessly, living life one day at a time and ignoring the gentle voice in my spirit beckoning me to find a better way to be a man. *Ummm, maybe later.* I was determined to find any functional spotlight that would make me feel worthy and bask in it.

Hide and Seek

When a group of us in the neighborhood formed a musical band, the plume of smoke drifted into the lungs of our members. We were named "Nature's Balance," a South Bronx, New York 10-piece ensemble who somehow convinced ourselves that we were destined to be the next "Earth, Wind, and Fire." Their bass guitar player (Verdeen White) was the energetic performer whom I chose as my example. Oh, I had the look: white denim, bell-bottomed pants with a matching tapered jacket, platformed shoes, and a big ol' "Cisco Kid" style hat with a brim wide enough to conceal my red, weed-infused eyes. I played that bass, but nowhere close to the talent level of Verdeen, and far from able to provide the sustainable rhythm needed to help us make it to Madison Square Garden. In fact, we never even made it out of the rehearsal studio. Too much puff & stuff was going on up in there! Let's just toss that endeavor in the graveyard along with my other aspirations that gave up the ghost.

Through it all, the smoke was still plaguing me and confounding my judgments. My predictable routine included going to work, coming home, hanging out with my friends and getting high on that same bench I used to sit on while waiting for my dad to come. The monotonous cycle was beginning to annoy me until that Friday evening in early August of 1974. (Get ready for this one.)

Pulling in from work, I see my friends waiting by the bench for me to arrive as usual. The weekend had officially begun, it was payday, and they were waiting for me to go upstairs so I could come back down to start the festivities. Before going into the apartment, I stopped off at a neighbor's place to buy a $60 ounce of marijuana which was to be my contribution for the gathering. I'd been back home living with mom since my discharge from the Navy the prior year, and she was home at the time. After taking my shower and changing clothes, I overheard the news on the TV with another follow-up of the big story that rocked the nation the day before. Richard Nixon had resigned from the presidency in the aftermath of the Watergate scandal. As if that wasn't enough, we were constantly hearing about the global recession; odd and even refueling days at the gas pumps along with a speed limit reduction to conserve fuel; tornadoes in the U.S. and Canada; bombings in Britain; a Smallpox epidemic in India; and so on.

My steps toward the front door slowed to a halt while my brain was showered with a dismal forecast. Within minutes I was overwhelmed with a picture of an eroding society and the fallibility of mankind. I experienced a sensation that to this day is hard to explain. The next thing I remember was motioning my mom to come over to me as I stood in the bathroom and flushed the newly purchased marijuana down the toilet. I looked at her and said, "I can't do this anymore." She immediately hugged me and expressed how happy she was for me. She asked what happened and I told her that the world's events concerned me enough to make a change. She hugged me again.

When I went outside (empty-handed) to meet up with my friends and explained to them what I had just done, a hush fell over the small but intense crowd. Before the assorted words of disbelief came my way, I discovered that there is not much distinction between the facial expression of a person who is under the influence of marijuana, and that of a person who has just been told they were not going to be "served" any. They're both blank, "deer in the headlights" type of stares without the accompaniment of bodily motion. The mixture of comments included, "Are you kidding me?", "You flushed sixty dollars down the toilet?", "Why didn't you give it to me?"

I do remember answering that last question by saying, "If I thought it was bad for **me**, what kind of friend would I be to give it to **you?**" That answer didn't register as what any of them would consider to be reasonable or satisfying. At least, for the moment it didn't seem that way. But after the barrage continued for a little while longer, I spotted a face amidst the group that had a different look. It was a face of curiosity. One that suggested he wanted to understand what I experienced.

When things settled down a little, he approached me and said, "Let's take a walk." This was my comic book exchange buddy, Roland. As kids I lived in the apartment directly above his and we had an amusing system for trading. When either of us wanted to get the other's attention he'd tap on the radiator, and we'd meet at the windows. I would then lower a string for him to tie his comic book on, pull it up, tie mine on, then lower it down to him. No "funnies" that night, though. That evening was about serious business, so he asked me to walk with him and tell him what was going on. Our rap session took place as we walked around the elementary school that was near our apartment building. By now night had fallen and the moon and stars were illuminated brilliantly across the sky. Once again, I felt like the Lord was using His celestial display to get my attention, so I seized the opportunity to begin our talk.

"Just look at that sky, Roland," I said. "There's a God out there, and I believe He wants me to do better things with my life than smoke it away."

He agreed, and we had a nice, long conversation. Moving forward, my aim was to get to know God as never before by attending church and reading the Bible. Where should I start? I wanted to find a place where there was more teaching than preaching; a church where vociferous outcries weren't mandatory for everyone in attendance. Okay, I have an idea. There's a family that lives in my building and goes to services every week. They seem nice and mild-mannered, and if their church is anything like them, I should fit in very well. That's it...I'll approach them!

The next time I ran into the husband/father of that family I struck up a conversation with him. I felt comfortable asking him how I would be able to study the Bible since my challenge was getting past the seemingly archaic language in which it was written. He quickly assured me that I would benefit from using the Bible that his family and congregation used because it was a version penned in modern language that was very easy to understand. I was excited and for the first time in years I felt free from the "smoke" that marred my sight and dulled my senses.

Remarkably, I didn't miss it at all, but it took a while to completely distance myself from the people, places, and things that reminded me of my not-so-distant past. A few days after my initial meeting with that neighbor, he gifted me with my new Bible. He was right! The words were easily understandable which made for an effortless reading experience. I soon became aware of the "denomination" his family was affiliated with, and it wasn't long before I came to understand why they were not part of orthodox Christianity. When I found out that the group that I was getting involved with had radically different beliefs, I proceeded with caution. Something just didn't seem right, but I continued to attend the meetings and read their version of the Bible.

At 25 years old there was still much that I had to learn, but some of those lessons blindsided me and I ended up getting married to one of the members within only one year of being in the "organization." That's when things began to cave in. On board Naval warships an announcement would come over the ship's inboard speakers whenever we were approaching a storm. "Stand by for heavy rolls" was our warning to strap things down and secure ourselves because the waters were about to get rough. And that they did!

For "Bitter" or for "Worst"

There was an old *"Odd Couple"* episode in which Felix reluctantly allowed Oscar to teach him how to be sloppy for the sake of winning back his ex-wife. For those who remember that sitcom—and this episode in particular—you're beginning to laugh already. When Oscar pulled out all the stops and finally dumped a pile of trash on his phobic roommate, Felix sat traumatized in a state of shock with a frozen glance on his face that was hilarious. That would best describe the emotional paralysis I was in during (and after) a wedding that should have been stopped months before it occurred. Felix's distress was funny, mine was far from it!

We all know that there are two sides to every story. However, this story was so lopsided (and so long ago) that the details are not worth exposing. Rather than mentioning the personal aspects of all that occurred, the focus is on the "system" behind it all. This was—and apparently still is—a group who have been indoctrinated and corralled by an upper echelon of leaders stemming from founders who were proven to be false prophets and ill-equipped Bible translators. What's more, the identities of the ones who were behind the retranslation are withheld from its followers by using the excuse that they choose to remain humbly anonymous, so that God alone would receive full glory for the rewriting of the Scriptures.

Following a transitory exposure to false teachings and behaviors inconsistent with their outward portrayal, I walked—or should I say, **ran**—away from that association and the 367-day toxic marriage that threatened my well-being.

It's tormenting encounters like these that scream for a father's guidance before, during, and after the occurrence. A dad's God-inspired advice and leadership should be the signet to a son's authentication. It supplements the confidence he needs in order to trust his own decisions. Without it, it's like plucking the needle from a compass and sending a youngster off to find his way out of a dense, dangerous forest in the middle of the night. No, dad's mentorship isn't foolproof, but part of it can surely be used as a sensor to help steer you away from the hazards of getting involved with some bad elements out there who can mean more harm than good.

"Come have a seat, son. Let's kick it around." The value in that invitation could be the beginning of a whole new and exciting journey for a willing father-son team! This means no cell phones, game controllers, cans, bottles, or rolled-up intoxicants that can distract from a good, old fashioned heart-to-heart conversation. I could only dream of having talks like that. Not only would it have made a huge difference in the bad choices I made along the way, but the lasting memories of such times spent together would be enough to carry me through and beyond this lifetime.

"Daddy's Home"

(Not as in *he's back*. Rather, *he's at his place whenever I would go by to see him.*)

It didn't take too long for me to head back to the cloud of delusion caused by marijuana. What's worse is that I became completely turned off to anyone and anything promoting the goodness of God. After all, my seeking Him was sincere, and He allowed me to get mixed up with a group of false purveyors of what they considered to be good news. I tried; it didn't work...moving on. I'm even going to see if it's too late to establish a relationship with my dad at this point. Not sure what that looks like, but I know where to find him and I'm pretty sure I know what he'll be doing.

As usual, I'd sit there, not knowing what to say or how to process what **he** was trying to say. Sometimes the clock on the wall appeared to be out of service as the time crept along. Often his wife consumed more alcohol than he did, but she was somehow able to handle hers better. She was the catalyst, controller, and constructor. His job was to just follow the game plans laid before him. He had a good heart, but I believe the drinking was a way to drown his sorrows from things in his life that went wrong while he was a soldier during World War II. Also, his father—I would later find out—was estranged from the family, so he missed out on the same things I did. (Are you beginning to see how this thing works?)

Occasionally, he would even attempt to make up for lost time by attending a couple of my softball games. Remember, he never made it to any of my Little League games; and now here he is, many years later, seeing me play as an adult on a very competitive level. It was easy to see the pride he felt on the evening when our team made it to the final round of the playoffs. Before the game I wasn't sure whether my nervousness was due to the pressure of the game, or from hoping he wouldn't show up tipsy. Everything turned out okay. We won the game, and he wasn't too out of sorts.

The more I saw him (and it really wasn't much) the more I wondered what compelled him to believe that living apart from our family was such a good decision. Were we that bad? Moreover, as a juvenile I often thought that if I had been a better bundle of joy he would have never left. Funny—but not really—how many nonsensical notions pass through the imagination of one whose heart has been fragmented.

A strong shift in the wind grabbed ahold of me and hit me with a profound reality. In a not so different way, I had become him! There, in his apartment, I would sit in a somewhat distorted manner, not really wanting to be there, unsure of what to say, with my mind preoccupied by whatever pleasures await me beyond that front door. No hard feelings or unforgiveness; I was just void of any strong desire to stick around.

"A Good Move"

My thrill really came when mom was there the night that we won the championship in that softball league. The problems she and I had with getting along before I went into the service was nothing but a faded memory as the distant oceans brought us closer together. From then on, we rode those waves of a loving connection throughout the years. It became crystal clear to me how many sacrifices she made for me and Denise, while trying to play the role of two parents. It's a shame that a youthful mind doesn't usually come to appreciate things like that until maturity sets in. Nevertheless, living back at home at good ol' building 308 was a pleasure!

Since Denise moved out a couple years before my enlistment with the Navy ended, it left just mom and me holding down the fort in apartment #5B. She was busy with her job at the phone company, and I was still working steadily at the bank. We coexisted very nicely and shared good laughing sessions until the wind of change blew in our direction. After living at that same address for 27 years, mom decided to move to another borough and upgrade to a nicer apartment, while I moved further north of the city after finding a nice place of my own. The transition was a good one for both of us and it caused me to segue into a new development.

My new apartment complex was very close to where my dad was living at the time. Although the proximity could allow for frequent visits, it didn't play out that way. My goal was still to discover my purpose, to find stability within myself, to shake the painful effects of not having a dad to grow up with, and to meet the woman I'd marry so that we could become the complete family I wished I had the pleasure of enjoying when I was a little boy. After all, that was my exact prayer and promise to God as a young son lamenting over his mom's agony. Little did I know that it would be best to have those first three objectives aligned before entering blissful matrimony!

Live and Learn

In our western culture, prearranged marriages are not customary. In fact, we see that as extremely risky primarily because we'd have to entrust our parents to make a wise (and tasteful) decision that would not be disastrous for us. When you think about it, even our own selections produce bad results sometimes. So, what system should we be using?

Might I suggest that our methodology needs to lean more towards using a standard based on qualities that include an **inward appeal** rather than just a superficial attraction.

Being in a good position to have a better chance of choosing the right spouse benefits every young man whose dad spends time teaching him what to look for in a woman. At the same time, he delights in allowing himself to be a prime example of what his daughter should be seeking in a man. Without this type of tutelage, they can end up in a hit-or-miss aimless search that results in a lot of wasted time and crippled emotions. Those of you who have been down that road—and statistics prove that all too many have—you know that it can be exhausting and heartbreaking.

****Dads: Sit down with your children and talk to them. Be creative and make the process fun yet instructive. Maybe even do some zany role-playing! Open arms and open conversations work wonders and will build bridges that can span across generations. Your words will be like priceless gems deposited in their treasure chest of memories and have lasting value.*

By now it's obvious that I wish my father could have been my coach in this area too. I must say, though, that for me dating was more of a search than a playground. My intent was to meet a lady whose principles came as close as possible to mine. Of course, physical attraction was important to me, but after seeing her "house" I needed to see who was at "home." Sounds too demanding? It would seem like it, but not if you consider that I understood that to get quality you'd have to bring quality.

And **that's** where I struggled. Remember, I suffered from low self-esteem due to the deficiencies cited earlier. To make matters worse, the smoke in my eyes had figuratively impaired my vision, along with my ability to make sound judgments. It had just latched itself onto me and hung on like a backpack. I made a weak attempt at talking myself into believing that if I met a woman who indulged herself in the same pastime, we would be a good fit for each other. But fortunately, I must have had a trace of common sense left because I didn't want a relationship that was void of sobriety. Sitting around in a fog as a couple wouldn't have been my idea of a good time, especially since I didn't even enjoy doing it anymore. Hmmm...that would be merely existing like a couple that I was very familiar with but did not want to replicate!

The more things changed, the more they stayed the same. Whatever happened to those strong promptings I felt years prior? You know, the harvest moon that night at sea; the sudden urge to flush an expensive portion of marijuana down the toilet; the setting out to find God and learn what His plan was for my life. Was it all happenstance, or was it a divine calling that I was running from?

Maybe I just need more proof.

In time—as if time was something I could control—God might pay another visit and speak a little louder or longer. I heard often enough that He is our Heavenly Father. That sounded good and I believed that He was out there, but "there" was just too far away. I needed someone more tangible - someone whose attention I wouldn't have to share with a gazillion other people in the world.

My dad only has two children, and he can't even care for **them**, so how can I trust a God Who is responsible for a countless number of children? I can't sit on that bench and wait for any more buses (or chariots). If He was coming for me, please come. And if He was trying to tell me something, His voice was going to have to resonate like a sonic boom. Until then, I would live by sight and continue to be a good person (whatever that is). I was going to put faith in my own instincts and keep it moving. When the smoke cleared—or when the bus arrived—maybe God will be standing there. If not, well...we'll see.

***

This would be a very good time to insert your bookmark and either take a break or turn out your nightlight and retire for the evening. The phrase, "the plot thickens" is especially applicable here, so you'll probably want to be alert for all that comes next.

6

About Face, About Grace

What ever happened to the Boogeyman? We're all familiar with how Dracula, Frankenstein, and the Mummy all met their demise, but I don't recall hearing about the Boogeyman ever being apprehended or slain. That evasive monster was so shadowy that his vagueness made him even more frightening. I believe he had a counterpart too - The Sandman.

As naïve kids, we were told that the Sandman would come and sprinkle sand in our eyes to make us go to sleep, but they never quite explained what the Boogeyman would do to us. We just knew that he wouldn't leave anything under our pillow like the Tooth Fairy would. (Now that I think about it, with a name like Boogeyman, I'm not so sure that I'd even **want** what he might leave under the pillow!) All I knew was that the threat of him coming to get me if I didn't go to sleep made it almost impossible to go to sleep, especially with no Superdad at home for protection.

That type of security was a mere figment of my imagination. Mom was a tough cookie, although I didn't think she could go the distance with any of my most dreaded monsters. Still, —like most "project moms"—she had no problem coming outside or to our school to confront anyone who caused me or my sister any trouble. She did an excellent job of providing the security that made us feel safe in her care, but even as a young boy I felt as though something was out of order. Dads don't necessarily need to have a threatening presence or image to act as a deterrent to danger or harm. Just being there with valor and confidence in facing any situation brings a child to a sheltered place of comfort and serenity.

A New Beginning

I loved my new studio apartment! It was in an area that was home to many young and aspiring people. A big plus was being only a 45-minute commute away from my job, yet far away from the hustle and bustle of the big city once work was done. As I mentioned earlier, it wasn't very far from where my dad lived, so he and I had a few bonding sessions when he'd come over to help me get established. He did some painting for me and even treated me to some furniture, which was a tremendous contribution.

Once, I had apparently gotten sick from something I ate and spent the entire day from sunup until sundown vomiting, sweating, and in excruciating pain. He sat with me and monitored my condition before finally taking me to the emergency room at a nearby hospital. There, I was diagnosed with food poisoning and slept it off before feeling better the next morning. The circumstances were extremely unpleasant, to say the least, but it can still go on record as time spent together. Funny, though—but not really—that was a long sought-after father-son moment that was wasted on a sick visit. Oh well, I'll take whatever I can get.

Despite my not adhering to strong Christian values at the time, my bachelor pad was not used as what would be called a "den of iniquity." It was primarily a hangout for my card-playing buddies, Sunday afternoon and Monday Night Football friends, and a place for me to enjoy my own solitude while still ensnared by that same weed-smoking habit. There were units all around me but fortunately the walls were not thin, so it was perfect for quiet times of thinking about life's strategies. It wasn't much of an effort for me to meet new friends in my building and throughout the neighborhood, which included a family across the hall. They were a mother and two daughters, one of which was a high school senior, the other about 21 years old. The three were very pleasant and had a noticeably close relationship until tragedy blindsided them. The mom was diagnosed with pancreatic cancer, and she expired rapidly, leaving the girls bewildered and overwhelmed with grief. I, along with other surrounding neighbors, rallied around them and doled out heaping portions of compassion and support. As the months rolled by, they were functioning much better, and the older sister was excited when she landed what she considered to be a great job. Meanwhile, the younger sister graduated from high school and attended a local college while continuing to live at home. Things seemed to be moving in the right direction for them, at least for the time being.

Big sis met a coworker who courted her, and they were married within a year. The newlyweds occupied the apartment, and the younger sister moved out to live with their grandmother. I met her husband and he seemed to be a nice, quiet sort of man. However, I did find it a little strange that on one occasion when they invited me and some of the other neighbors over, he didn't socialize much. What's more, he stayed in their bedroom most of the time while the rest of us were mingling in the living room. Still, she seemed very happy with her new husband, and they led a private, seemingly peaceful life together in the apartment that she, her sister, and mom used to share together. Just as a footnote, theirs was also an upbringing without a dad in the picture. That would bear a meaningful significance when we look in on them a little later as new developments are factored into this portion of the story.

Rapid Fire Escape

Many of us can relate to home as being a place where we can retreat after working in an unpleasant atmosphere all day, especially on a Friday knowing that the weekend would be an extended reprieve. Reversely, sometimes it's the place of employment that acts as a getaway from a noxious home life where you dread to return. When you're fortunate enough to shuttle between two environments that are equally enjoyable, then that's awesome! Thus was the case during the season when I was promoted to a supervisory position at a bank's regional center in lower Manhattan, New York City. The hours were much different from what I was accustomed to working. I worked from 3pm to 11pm Monday thru Friday, and I now had to drive a considerable distance since I could no longer commute via subway and railroad due to the trains' unfavorable schedule. That's okay, I liked night driving back then, and the ride was great because I didn't have to contend with rush hour traffic. Our crew listened to music, sang, and laughed while we worked, took turns bringing in lunch (more like dinner) for each other, and balanced the workload when someone else's was more burdensome than the others. On our way out the door, we made it a habit of saying "peace and love" before heading home. Such a remarkable group!

It was a crisp Friday night in the fall, my favorite day of the week and my favorite season of the year. I just left my elite coworkers and was headed home to my fantastic apartment. I'm cruising on a traffic-free FDR Drive with good music on the radio. It doesn't get much better than this, I thought. After a few minutes it got much worse. I smelled smoke in the air and unsuspectingly dismissed it as something burning within the project development across the road. I continued to enjoy my music and my drive until I felt a bit warm, then hot, then suddenly in my rearview mirror there's a flame rising from behind my seat! Whoa! Pulling over onto the shoulder, I began fanning the flames with my jacket all in a losing effort.

Within about 1 minute, I gave up as the fire spread to the front seats. I reached quickly through the flame to grab my keys from the column, slammed the door, then ran to a safe distance across the highway and into a small crowd that had assembled from the neighborhood. The fire lit up the night sky as I heard the faint sound of fire engines getting louder as they neared the scene. The firefighters worked quickly to douse the flames while my gaze was fixed on the wreckage that was my vehicle just a short time ago. Amid the crowd of onlookers were the sensationalists whose chatter reeked with misinformation.

One asked another, "Did they make it out?" The other replied, "No, they're still in there!"

Meanwhile, I'm standing right beside them (and shaking my head). It's close to midnight by this time, but I managed to make it to a phone and call one of my friends to come and get me. I'm so glad that I was able to retrieve my keys from the steering column before the blaze reached full intensity or I would not have been able to get into my apartment. It was a long ride home, and an even longer night before daybreak. There I laid, staring at the ceiling in total disbelief. The shock factor was thicker than the smoldering of my charred Pontiac, but I must say that things could have turned out a lot worse for me especially if there was any truth to that person's claim that I was still in the car. Times were very tough without a car (especially with my commute to work).

It would be months before I was able to get another one and it was my dad and his wife who made it possible through their financial help. I was back in business once again!

A Thief in the Night

You'll be stunned beyond your wildest imagination to discover who the "thief" would be, but first things first. Work was still great, my coworkers were still the cream of the crop, and the convenience of being a motorist again felt wonderful! Perhaps I was a slow learner in those days because I continued to base my happiness on whatever circumstances kept me in the groove. But how many of you agree that the amusement park has a closing time and the rides won't accept your quarters after hours? It certainly appeared that way when my employment terminated unexpectedly! My termination was due to my sporadic absenteeism following a longer than anticipated healing period after undergoing foot surgery. It seems I was wearing the wrong cleats for too long while playing softball and it finally caught up with me. Oh, I had accrued plenty of sick time, but I depleted it after a while since my recuperation was extensive. So now I'm laid up at home with more time on my hands without an income.

The bills began to mount along with the aggravation, but the good news was that my foot was healing nicely. Soon I was up and about, and my job search efforts increased. I was cold-calling, responding to classified ads, sending out resumes, etc. I kept at it non-stop and did all I could to keep the landlord and bill collectors at bay. It looked like a breakthrough was about to occur when an employment agency came very close to arranging two interviews for me, but both resulted in dead ends. By now things got so tight that I had even considered reenlisting in the Navy, but I managed to talk myself out of it. How could all of this be happening? I am an honorably discharged veteran with a background in basic electricity and electronics, as well as supervisory experience in a data entry department and computer operations within a well-known banking firm. All of that didn't matter. It was nearing the eleventh hour, and my debtors wanted their money.

I managed to get a few interviews, but each letter of rejection began with the same word: "Unfortunately." Not only was this the first time I had experienced lasting unemployment, but it also ushered in an acute sense of rejection based on this episode and others like it from my past.

Hopelessness set in until one of my neighborhood friends introduced me to a new   neighbor. He spoke about a money-making opportunity for me that was sure to provide me some breathing room while my prolonged search for work ran its course. In my despair, I listened. He worked the evening shift in the men's section of a high-class department store. One of his duties was to ring up customers' purchases. Without going into detail, he offered to arrange for me to be an undetected shoplifter so that I could sell some stolen clothing items to get enough money to catch up on my bills.

Surely, I was bothered by the whole concept because it was the wrong thing to do, but that cartoon angel on my shoulder was the real hero who shouted at my conscience before drop-kicking the cartoon devil off my other shoulder, who had been whispering in my other ear. I gave the plot a thumbs down. Still, what disturbed me most is that it took me a day to mull it over before declining. I even beat myself up for a while just for thinking about participating in such a scheme. If my plight was to continue then so be it, but I was not about to compromise at least **that** portion of my values while making a bad situation much worse than I could ever imagine. With a debilitating confidence, I pressed into my job-hunting efforts looking, hoping—but not yet praying—for a breakthrough.

Love is in the Air

One of the most difficult things to do while frantically pursuing employment is keeping your mind occupied during those moments when you're in need of a break from the search. It's hard, though, because there's a fight against feeling like time is of the essence and no moments can be wasted. An "overthinker" (which is what I was frequently labeled) finds it very easy to snatch fleeting thoughts and reel them into a brain hungry for something to contemplate. That is exactly what I did when I got weary from my dilemma.

Maybe I should have done better during my junior and senior years in high school. In fact, let's go back further than that, back to elementary and junior high school when so many teachers said I had a knack for creative writing. I should have heeded the guidance of my mother and rode those encouragements right into college after which I'd at least have a bachelor's degree by now. Did I blow it? Have I missed out on the best opportunities for a stellar career and a chance to prove to myself (and to my father) that I succeeded even with my emotional handicap? Oh well, time to hit the "off" switch and go get something to eat.

I got in my car to take a drive in the cold night air. One of my favorite supermarkets was a 24-hour grocery store that was about 20 minutes away. I liked going there very late because during this troubling period I was going through, avoiding contact with people brought more solace than having to socialize, even if it was brief and superficial. I was starting to become a loner by choice. An "introverted" extrovert. Makes sense? To me it did. This simply meant that although I loved interacting with people, my comfort zone was a place where my shyness and insecurities welcomed seclusion. I know it's weird, but that's where I was.

My yearning that night was for a specific brand of imported pistachio nuts, and that store was the only place I knew of that sold them. My taste buds were very clear about the kind of snack I craved so I didn't hesitate to comply regardless of how nippy it was outside. The store was situated on the opposite side of the road, so I had to use the U-Turn lane provided. When I did, there was a young man standing next to his car blowing into his hands while trying to get warm. It appeared that his car had broken down and he needed help.

Without giving it a second thought, I pulled over and asked him what was wrong. He explained that he had gotten out of his car to "relieve" himself and got locked out. He went on to tell me that he was far from home but that he was able to contact his parents who were on their way with a spare key. Ok, that's good, but it's after midnight, it's freezing outside, and it would take quite a while for his folks to get to him. I told him where I was headed and that sometimes there's a patrol car hanging out in the store's parking lot. My plan was to inform the police of his predicament hoping that they'd either unlock the car or let him get warm inside their vehicle until his parents reached him. When I pulled into the store's lot there were no police in sight. It only took a couple of minutes to make my purchase, so I left and headed home.

Not long down the road I got to thinking about a Bible verse that states, "If you don't love your brother who you can see, how can you love God who you can't see?" (Something like that.) [1 John 4:20, paraphrased.]

It's not that I was consciously being defiant, but I did spend a moment reasoning that one can just look at that stranded motorist and know that we were not brothers because of our skin contrasts. Also, why would that Scripture just pop into my head when I was not in fellowship with God at that time?

Those two valid points had no bearing on what happened next. I spun my car around, went into a nearby gas station, and purchased a cup of hot chocolate to take back to the young man in trouble. By the time I returned, his parents had already arrived and had him sitting in their car with a blanket around him while his car was warming up. I gave them the hot chocolate, they thanked me, and I drove off.

The feeling that came over me can be easily explained, but the reason for it was beyond my comprehension because it didn't seem to fit the occasion. Almost immediately after pulling away I felt like God was pleased with me for reaching out to help someone in need. Why was I even thinking that? Yes, I believed in God, but let's face it, I hadn't been actively pursuing a relationship with Him and I had distanced myself from all church affiliations. All I know is that the comfort food I picked up from the store was still in a bag on the passenger seat next to me, while this strange and unique brand of "comfort food" called compassion had already satisfied my yearning.

It's Now or Never

Ironically, I was driving to get nuts one night, then felt like I was **going** nuts a few days later! The bills were now out of control, and I was in jeopardy of losing my apartment if I didn't find work soon. I came close to being interviewed twice, but they called me off as they opted to hire another candidate.

Although I'm beyond dejected at this juncture, I circled an ad for a computer operator in the newspaper and called to see if the position was still open. For the first time in a while there was a ray of hope when the lady on the phone informed me that they were still accepting applications. My excitement was a bit guarded due to the several times I got worked up, only to be let down. They scheduled an interview with me a couple days later and I must say it was very hard to remain guarded since things went so well. After our meeting (which was on a Wednesday) the manager told me that they still had more applicants to see, and that if I was to be considered they would call me on Monday. Here's where it got good. They called me the very next day and asked me to return for a 2nd interview on Friday. I didn't even have to agonize over the weekend wondering if I'd get offered a return visit!

Okay, man, calm down! Breathe. *Nope, I can't!*

I'm experiencing hope at a level that has been foreign to me for such a long time. Friday morning came and I was a mess. A **good** mess. More than being caught in a current of nervous excitement, was a sudden, irresistible urge to pray. Would God even listen to a prayer from a person who basically turned away from what little faith he had? So selfish of me, but I really needed Him at that moment, and as awkward as it was, I began praying for Him to end my nightmare and help me land this job. It's generally believed that whenever a 2nd interview is requested it usually means that it's a certainty that you've been approved.

Perhaps that was true in my case, but I prayed anyway for two reasons:

- I sensed a strong, indescribable prompting to appeal in a

manner that I hadn't done prior to applying for any of the other jobs.

- Twice before, a position looked promising, and it turned out to be a "crash and burn."

Then came the moment of truth. The follow-up meeting went extremely well, and I heard the words I was longing to hear: "We'd like to offer you the position."

No need to express how I felt, it's pretty much a no-brainer.

Since the following Thursday was Thanksgiving and the company was closed the day after, I was given the option to work the abbreviated week, or start on the following Monday. I chose the latter, giving myself a whole week to reconfigure and recuperate from my long period of unemployment. Going into the holiday season with a new job made it so much more celebratory while feeling as though the worst was behind me and the best was yet to come!

Part of the "best" was six days later. With the Macy's Thanksgiving Day Parade airing on TV, the thought of chowing down on mom's traditional spread in a few hours, and the security of an income on its way, I could have easily been riding one of the floats at the parade. As I was moving about my apartment getting ready for my drive and a fun-filled day, the sudden thought of what this special holiday represented hit me like a ton of bricks. It was far more than the turkey, parade, and all the extras attached. Giving thanks in this moment for my new beginning was something I felt compelled to do. I stopped in my tracks, dropped to my knees, and remembered to thank God for granting the request I had so desperately appealed to Him for only a few days ago. And then it happened.

For the first time in my life I experienced hearing directly from God! With a clear, majestic voice not in my ears but from within the very core of my being I felt Him say, **"All you had to do was ask."**

It seems so unfair to ask someone reading this to try to imagine the inexplicable sensation that overcame me, but please try anyway. When I "heard" that, I was so overcome by the certainty of His message and just knowing that He would visit me in that way, that I began to weep uncontrollably. I sat for a while to gather myself as even the acoustics in the room were affected by the authenticity of His presence. For sure, that was a Thanksgiving Day that I would never forget, but unfortunately—as human nature would have it—I retrogressed and continued on with a "business as usual" attitude once I settled back into my work-life rhythm.

It didn't take long for me to familiarize myself with the flow of my responsibilities but transitioning to solitary functioning was quite an adjustment. As the evening shift computer operator, my hours were 3pm-11pm. I was used to working those hours, but this was the first time I'd be doing it alone. That meant my interaction with coworkers only lasted for about two hours since everyone else in the company clocked out at 5pm. Come to think of it, I didn't even see my friends much anymore. By the time I got off, they were home and asleep in preparation for the next day's "normal" working hours, and when their day was finished, I was on the job. I was forced to become a loner; a solo act who was still puffing on those "illusion sticks." Whatever happened to my humble, thankful experience in the presence of God not long before? I didn't realize it at first, but I had done what I grew accustomed to doing whenever He would get me out of a jam.

Unawares, I was saying "Thanks, God...I'll take it from here."

Storm Clouds Rolling In

I ran into my young neighbor in the hallway after seeing very little of her over the past year. It was around the time she and her husband were celebrating their 1st anniversary, so I wished her a happy one. Interestingly, her response was non-verbal, but her facial expression spoke volumes. It wasn't one that told me she was happy. I was in a hurry, and it appeared as though she was too, so all I could say was, "We'll talk." About a week later after coming home from work one night—and remember, it's very late—there's a knock at my door. It was my neighbor's husband who asked if I had a minute for him to show me something. I followed him to their apartment and was in shock at what I saw. Their whole place had been ransacked! Things were in total disarray and before I could utter a word, he told me that this was his wife's doing. He went on to tell me that they hadn't been getting along and that she decided to leave him. Apparently, she did it while he was at work, and this is how he found things when he returned. I asked him what he was going to do, and he said that he wanted to find her and bring her home. Okay, it sounded like a plan of reconciliation. I'm all for that!

While circling my neighborhood in search of a parking spot several nights later I happened to spot the couple walking down the street holding hands. Being happy to see that they were reunited, I honked and waved as I drove by. Oddly, neither of them waved back at me. He just kind of looked and turned away. After giving it a second glance, I noticed that although they were holding hands, her reluctant stride hinted that she wasn't really into the moment. The scene resembled a parent leading a pouting child by the hand while the child clearly doesn't want to go along.

Anyway, I didn't give it much further thought until two nights later. That's when the husband called me while I was at work to tell me that his wife was dead!

I was speechless for a few seconds but then said, "I just saw you two the other night! What happened?" He answered, "That wasn't her, that was a coworker I was walking with."

Okay, I was not sure how to process that without questioning my own sanity. I was in too much shock to press the issue. He explained that she was found shot to death and floating in the river along the same roadway where my car caught fire not very long before. Such a tragedy! Two laid back, nice people who had only been married a little over a year; mom passed away suddenly months before that, and now this.

Things took an even uglier turn when I'm coming in once again from work (I should've taken a day job) only to find the husband sitting in the hallway with a security guard. When he saw me approaching, he told me that he was a suspect in his wife's murder. Meanwhile, the police were raiding his apartment looking for clues. Even then he seemed more sad than nervous. I suppose he should have been a bit concerned because a few days later I saw in the newspaper where he was arrested—then, later convicted—of the murder. This was melodramatic beyond my wildest description! There was too much stuff happening around me, and the realization that I was a helpless "cast member" in this script weighed heavily on me.

What's next? I'm not sure I wanted to know.

The Lost and Found

By now I was in a daze and a haze at the same time. My routine consisted of working, coming home to a quiet, empty apartment, and getting high by myself. The days, weeks, and months passed while through a succession of misunderstandings, some of my friendships began to fade away. Something strange was happening, and I couldn't put my finger on it. The guys would still come over some weekends for our football game gatherings and that was fun for a while, but much of my time was spent in my unaccompanied surroundings.

It's one thing to be alone and another to be lonely. Oh yeah, I was single with a good job, a friendly personality, and told on more than one occasion that I was "pleasing to the eyes," but even with a nice bachelor pad the only field I played was on the softball field. You see, somewhere not too deeply embedded within me was the desire to be married with a family. More than that, I wanted to have the traditional type of family with mom and dad **together** in the home, and the children secure and happy because of us. For that reason, I'd wait it out and not waste time and energy on meaningless dating. Call it old-fashioned, but my desire was to be called "Papa" rather than "Playa."

Through that providential pause there were a couple of distant friends out there who were trying to get me to read some Bible-based tracts and attend church, but I was not receptive. Then, I came across an offering on TV. It was a book titled "Power for Living." In it was an explanation of how God not only gives us the power to live, but to live that life abundantly. With hesitation and interest at the same time, I called the phone number on the screen for my free copy.

When it arrived and I began to read it, I was drawn immediately to three sports celebrities whose testimonies compelled me to sit up and take notice. They were Tom Landry, former coach of the Dallas Cowboys; Julius ("Dr. J") Erving, basketball superstar of the Philadelphia 76ers, and Steve Bartkowski, quarterback for the Atlanta Falcons. The enlightenment of how they had a personal relationship with Jesus Christ was far different than an exhortation regarding the importance of church attendance and membership. What really made their witnessing efforts so much more effective was the way they conducted themselves during their contests. I wasn't too familiar with Steve Bartkowski, but I had seen Dr. J and Tom Landry often enough to notice an easy-going, "always in control" type of demeanor. When I learned of their spiritual connection with (and their love for) God, I said, "So **that's** what it is about them!" Their words were backed by their actions, and it made all the difference in the world!

For the first time, I was made to understand that it was more about a relationship rather than a religion. That was the game-changer!

When life's serendipities come together and begin to roll around in one's thoughts, there's no choice but to suspect that all events (some good, some bad) were on a mission to bring a special moment into focus. For such a time as then and for a purpose yet to be defined, that is exactly what happened after reading that book. Somehow, some way, a change was needed.

History was repeating itself as I began to reflect on that summer evening many years before when I sought the Lord after flushing the marijuana down the toilet. In the whirlwind of my contemplations were the many years of disappointments, close calls, bad choices, and misdirected ambitions. On the other hand, I had to factor in a sense of divine protection, hope, and God's whispers via the wonder of a harvest moon on the horizon in the middle of the Mediterranean Sea, and the assurance of His comforting voice of grace on that very special Thanksgiving morning.

As Kenny Loggins would melodically say *"This is It...Your Back's to the Corner."* I wouldn't be a fool anymore!

It was New Year's Eve, 1983, and moments away from the big ball dropping in Times Square, New York. I was at home alone as the countdown began: *5...4...3...2...1...Happy New Year!!!* It was now 1984, and by the grace of God I made it! Yeah, I made it, but I had a strange hunch that I might not get to say that in 365 days unless I surrendered my life to the One Who gave it to me.

While the climactic festivities continued on the TV screen, I prayed a very poignant and repentant prayer. Although I was full of remorse and poured out my grief from a contrite heart, I admitted that all the spiritual "salesmen" out there had left me confused.

Not sure what (or who) to believe, I said, "Jesus, if You are who You say You are, I need You now."

At first, I thought that doubt might nullify my petition, but then I remembered reading somewhere where God said to come as you are. That freed me to believe that my prayer of salvation was honored. The floor didn't shake, no smoke filled the room, and no faint harpsichord music played in the background. There wasn't even a hint of a mystical ambience. All I know is that I had entered a covenant with the Almighty and I felt guaranteed that my life had changed forever!

Although I still struggled with smoking marijuana for a few weeks after my conversion, I truly believed that I was about to make my escape from it. That was proven when out of the blue a friend I hadn't seen in six years called me and wanted to get together. I went to pick him up and was so glad to see him. We then went to another friend's place, and I felt like a fish out of water while the "peace pipe" was passed around among us.

The atmosphere was the same, as was the paraphernalia and aimless banter. Nothing had changed, except me! When I drove him home, he iced the cake for me. You see, he had been incarcerated for a while, which left him uncertain about a brighter future. I explained that although I hadn't been institutionalized, I was in a different kind of bondage, nonetheless. My offering of encouragement to him was that we had a choice to either wallow in our past or pick up the pieces and look forward to better days ahead. I had hoped that my words inspired him to move in a positive direction, but the very next week proved otherwise.

My friend across the complex called and said, "Come on over, the council is here." He wouldn't tell me who was there or what was going on, but I went anyway. I arrived to find a few buddies I used to hang out with, including the same one from the week before. This was my big test. They had a "smorgasbord" of substances that at one time would have excited me. However, I had no desire at all to participate, nor was there even the slightest temptation! I sat with them for a while and was amazed that at one time in the not-so-distant past I was a prominent member of that assemblage.

> *"There, but for the grace of God, go I."* [2]
>
> John Bradford

I drank water, I watched, I listened, and I left. The next day was Superbowl Sunday, and here we go again. This time I was at a different location, but the activity was the same. I don't remember who played in that game, but I felt like I was the real winner. After years of being ensnared and gripped by a substance dependency I was finally free!

That Superbowl was played on January 22, 1984, and it was mom's birthday. I should have spent the day with her so that we could celebrate her birthday and my deliverance at the same time. That would have been more fitting especially since she had also given her life to Christ two or three years before I did. What made that day even more amazing is that it was the last time I would see, smell, or even witness the remnants of a marijuana event. Allow me to substantiate that claim.

> *At the time of this writing, it has been 39 and ½ years. Let's try that again...***14,409 days** *since God totally removed every trace of marijuana from my midst!!!*

I believe beyond the shadow of a doubt that He wanted to not only rescue me from marijuana, but He wanted to put His miracle-performing power on display for me as a parting gift! From then onward, when I'd see a sign on someone's property which reads, "Keep Off The Grass," it means so much more than just a request to not mess up the lawn by walking on it. It is a reminder of how messy one's life can become by treading on areas that are more like minefields rather than attractive walkways. I was no stranger to eye-opening encounters, but this time things were quite different. There's no turning back!

7

Now What?

Along with a newly isolated, substance-free lifestyle came an unhealthy eating habit that took me a minute to get under control. Coming home late after work usually sent me straight to the kitchen. Things like fried chicken, chocolate chip cookies, potato chips, or ice cream in front of the TV at 1am were all part of my new normal. It got to the point where I couldn't fall asleep unless my belly was filled with a buffet of junk-food delectables. This night I grabbed cookies and milk and got busy with them. They tasted good going down, but it was a setup for either a weird dream, insomnia, an upset stomach, or heartburn. Looks like the weird dream would be the winner, so away we go!

Zzzzzz...

It's the first day of school. I climbed aboard that bright yellow bus and figured out why they chose that color. It's the happy color! It's the one that makes us feel like school is going to be an awesome experience and that education is fun. I sat in my seat looking out the window, carefully avoiding socializing with those around me for fear that the other students might detect my apprehension. I couldn't help noticing that those seated—as well as the ones boarding—appeared to be as timid as I was. I mean, why not? It was our first day, and things looked so much different now that we were all grown up. Okay, I get it. Playtime was over and life's lessons were about to be hurled at us like never before. No more messing with toys and squandering valuable time daydreaming or goofing around with friends. I was on that bus now headed to a place of higher learning. Well, at least higher than I had experienced. I wondered, though…with a day as important as this, why didn't one of my parents wait with me at the bus stop and wave to me with teary eyes as we pulled off? It was no surprise that dad wouldn't be there, since it was clear to me that he had a problem with buses, but why wasn't mom there? Then again, I suppose it would have looked a little odd since I was almost 33 years old by then!

The school I was heading to didn't follow an elementary level curriculum. Indeed not. This form of higher learning would involve an exquisite education that covered how this universal tale began, where it's heading, and all points in between. Through the inspired teachings of some of the best instructors that history has ever known, I would discover a deeper part of myself and what my purpose on this earth was intended to be. The names of some of my assigned teachers were kind of familiar to me because they were a spinoff from the historical figures whose stories were used to enhance our learning experience. Their reputations preceded them, their credentials validated them, and I heard that their students' success rates were off the charts! Being mindful of all this impressive information made it easier for me to feel good about the studies that were up ahead. Still, I was a bit nervous and wished that this would be the one time that my dad would have seen me off.

Seriously, dude…get over it!

When the bus arrived at the school, I began to gather my thoughts in addition to my belongings. Each step took me further from my seat, but closer to the fresh start I needed. As I exited the bus, I saw something in front of me that caught my eye, grabbed my heart, and pulled a powerful gasp of breath from my lungs.

In amazement, I saw an image of my Dad sitting on the bench! He was waiting for me to arrive and was holding a sign much like the driver of a car service displays at the airport when he's picking up a passenger. The sign simply read, "Son." Tears welled up in my eyes when it suddenly hit me. While I had spent so much time anxiously waiting on that bench for my father, it was my **Heavenly** *Father Who was waiting patiently for me! He was longing for my submission and for my repentance from the things that kept me estranged from Him for a very long time. He gathered the best teachers whose experiences were documented via biblical accounts and brought me to them for the purpose of my in-depth nourishment.*

I was finally ready, willing, and (by His Amazing Grace) able to receive the proper training needed for my growth and development so that I could finally live a meaningful, purposeful life that would make Him the proud Dad that I pined for. Gotta go; the bell is about to ring!

Forgiveness

My very first class was taught by a teacher who went by the name Joseph. He led us through an incredible biblical tale about forgiveness. In the Bible, Joseph was the 11th son born to Jacob and shared the same mother (Rachel) with his younger brother, Benjamin. At only 17 years old his father saw wisdom in him well beyond his age, which resulted in his being favored by his dad over his older brothers. Their jealousy of him led to such an intense hatred that they plotted to kill him. But instead, they sold him into slavery. He ended up being promoted to a lead position inside the captain of the guard's house, as his integrity was evident because of his noticeable walk with God.

A huge problem for him developed when his refusal to give in to temptation due to the captain's wife's persistent sexual advances stirred her ire, thus prompting her to accuse him falsely of rape. That allegation landed him in jail. There, too, he was granted favor by the keeper of the jail because the Lord was with him and **for** *him. It continued to get better as he was elevated to 2nd in command under Pharaoh over all of Egypt after being able to interpret the King's dream and devise an ingenious plan to help the land thrive during an impending famine.*

Fast-forwarding through the story brings us to when his brothers—unaware of who he was—humbled themselves before him to purchase food for the family.

Later, Joseph revealed himself to his brothers who had wronged him, and it was an emotional reunion. Being in such a high position of authority he could have easily retaliated in brutal fashion. Instead, he forgave them, loved on them, and provided for them. That is a capsulized version of the story. The practical application is as follows:

The absence of a father leaves a wound that often doesn't heal easily or completely. For some of us the pain has been excruciating at times, while on better days we may only feel a dull ache. There is also a contingency of those whose dads were abusive to them and caused a lot of damage to their children, and to the household overall.

In every varying scenario, we have come to a place where forgiveness stands before us with a raised eyebrow asking, "Are you going to let me into your heart?" And we should. In fact, it is crucial to our prayer life – as well as the fact that we were granted forgiveness from God for the sins we've committed, and commit continuously against Him (see Matthew 6:15). Right then our teacher, Mr. Joseph, invited all hurting students to agree with him in the following prayer:

> *Lord God, in Your Divine omniscience, You understand the painful journey that it has been without my dad being there to help me along the way. Often, I have struggled to make wise decisions, to appreciate my own worth, and sometimes to share substantial contributions with those in need around me. Recklessly I've sought after the approval from some objectionable people who have led me astray and caused me to suffer hardships and harsh consequences. As I ask Your forgiveness for my iniquities, I sincerely forgive my dad for not fulfilling his duties as a father*

who would provide the guidance, love, and protection that I so desperately needed. If he is in Your presence right now, please let him know that I release him from any shame or blame toward him that I may have held in my heart because of his absence. If he is still walking among us, please bless him and give him peace in knowing that I forgave him, and that all is well with my soul. It is with praise and thanksgiving to You that I offer this prayer in the name of Jesus Christ, my forgiving Savior...Amen.

Perfect timing! Off to my next class titled Domestic "Ark"itecture. Hmmm...I wonder what that's about.

The True Measurement of a Man

The instructor introduced himself as Mr. Noah and told the class that he would be sharing some tips on not only starting a family, but on how to cultivate and provide for a family. He went on to explain how the first steps should be those that bring us to a close walk with God. By doing so, we establish an intimate relationship which leads to a firm belief in not only recognizing God's voice, but an undeniable trust in His directives even when they don't seem to make sense. Mr. Noah highlighted a few essential components that help fortify a family's structure and keep it sturdy enough to withstand the fiercest storms imaginable.

He stressed repeatedly the importance of striving to be a man who would walk uprightly with the Lord, while attaining a respectful and noble character among the people of his community. I must confess that my overactive imagination hadn't changed much in the past years. My tendency has often been to drift off during a lecture, and this day was no exception. While Mr. Noah spoke of things like closeness with God, family construction, and good character before men, I couldn't help but think about the interesting link between his name and the builder of the biblical ark.

*That faithful saint of ancient times was recorded as being **righteous** before God, **blameless** amid an evil society, and **trusted** to carry out a mind-boggling task with **patience** and **endurance.** His hard labor lasted for many years without even the slightest hint of an impending doom upon the earth. What's more, he had to supply enough food for his family and all the animals aboard the vessel, and set an example of great leadership for his three sons to follow.*

We have come a long way since the building of Noah's Ark. Although the Bible mentioned the exact measurements that he was to use to construct an ark that would conform to the specifications given, there is no indication of the type of instrument he used to ensure accuracy. What we do know is that Noah was obedient and that he filled the order explicitly for a solid, waterproof seacraft. If he didn't, the floating household wouldn't have survived the onslaught of the watery catastrophe.

*Likewise, God used His own device to determine the true characteristics of the kind of man he required for such a tremendous undertaking. The **length** of this special servant would be proportionate to the patience he'd need to build the ark, and to wait for the chosen time when it would be sealed and lifted high above the earth. His **width** represented the tender care he put into assembling the animal compartments and making comfortable living conditions for his family. As for his **height,** a godly stature is what Noah already had in the first place, which is why he was chosen to be the start of a new civilization.*

The good qualities He looked for in Noah are the God-like qualities a man needs to possess when building a modern-day ark for his family. Having those components will contribute to a formidable home designed to cultivate love, unity, and shield against harsh attacks that the evil one sends its way.

I returned covertly from my daydream and rejoined the class as Mr. Noah spoke of the brand of husband/father that all men should strive to be. Merging into the traffic of his monologue took me back to the juvenile vow that I made to God in that prayer of promise when I was a little fella. Oh yeah, I'll be ready when that time comes. I will try my best—which will certainly be sufficient with God leading me—to be the "Noah" of my family. Perfection will not be in me, but I'll be a patriarch devoted to honoring the Lord as He trusts me to serve them under His guidance. Knowing how I felt without that kind of dad in my home made me even more determined to protect my children from the same deficiencies that I suffered from then, and, sometimes, even now. Great class, Mr. Noah...well done!

Strong Leadership

*Such an interesting segue into my next period since my zeal for wholesome fathering and "husbanding" has me chomping at the bit. While the epitome of leadership is through the example of Jesus Christ as Son of God, **and** as Son of Man, there was a notable representation of a powerful leader bearing the same name as the instructor of my next class. Professor Rod Moses was a "staff" member in that he was a teacher hired to lead students toward greater achievements. By contrast, the Moses of the Old Testament was a "staff" member too, but a different kind. He carried a staff that symbolized God's presence—in addition to His signs and wonders—while he led a nation out of bondage under God's direction. It is the life and leadership of the biblical Moses whom the modern educator of this class brought into focus as an example of what a genuine trailblazer of the home looks like.*

When Moses was drawn to a non-consumable burning bush, he heard the voice of Almighty God speaking to a man lacking confidence. Moses' assignment was to lead God's chosen people, the Israelites, out of captivity and into the land promised to Abraham's descendants. But before doing that, his job was to go before Pharaoh of Egypt and demand their release – which took tremendous courage. Again, this was a man who was not only insecure, but he had a speech problem also. God assured Moses that he would not have to do it alone. The Lord Himself would be with him and would empower him with the words to speak to the Egyptian King and to the elders of Israel. That's all it took! That's all it ever takes...the unfaltering confidence in knowing that God goes before us, works through us, and watches our back at the same time.

***Dads: C'mon dads, you can do this! Doubtless it can be a bit overwhelming to think of how much you are depended on to lead your family through the wilderness of life. You are called on to be the leader, strategist, guard, provider, mentor, and arbitrator. They say, "A woman's work is never done," but a man's work is seldom fun. Nevertheless, when following the Lord's lead and instructions, your efforts to be the ensign bearer of your family will not go unnoticed, even when it appears to be unappreciated. The necktie that you get for Father's Day sometimes has a hidden meaning. While you may see it as a simple "default" present given without any thought behind it, think of it as the family's way of saying, "You have all you need because God has put a special blessing on you by giving you the gift of family." Someday that plain and ordinary gift will become like pure gold. For now, be like Moses and lead. Willingly accept God's commission to be the kind of father and husband that would make Him and your loved ones proud. Your children will have an easier trek to the promised land and they will not have to wander aimlessly in the wilderness of a challenged society without your leadership. You are the man because God **made** you to be one, and you are a father because He has **blessed** you to be one. Now, be a dad because your children **need** you to be one. There's no time like the present, and no present like the precious time that you can spend with them.

Solemn Man

Each class thus far has provided an inspiring walkway for my new journey. Judging from the title of my last class of the day, I sensed that it would be powerful enough to have a lasting impact on everything I'd be involved in for the rest of my life. Many of us would like to think that we are equipped instinctively with wisdom. However, even before entering this next classroom I already knew the distinction between being wise and being a "wise guy." Or, one who is smart as opposed to one who is a "smart aleck." Guilty as charged; at times I have outslicked myself and ended up on the desolate side of wisdom's compensations.

Note to Self: *Go into this room with great expectations, and hopes of good things to follow because you have a heart filled with praise and honor for the One who granted you a new beginning and a chance to live an abundant life. And while doing so, remember the verse written in Proverbs 1:7 (ESV, paraphrased) that reads, "The fear (or reverence) of the Lord is the beginning of knowledge." It is with the acquisition of knowledge—and proper application of it—that wisdom becomes interwoven throughout a person's nature and character. Yeah, bring it on, Professor Weisman...I'm front and center, and ready for a heavy dose!*

We all filed in with somewhat muffled chatter and took our seats as the Professor sat on the edge of his desk watching us. He didn't greet us as we entered, nor did he show any facial expressions or body language that suggested that he was happy to have us in his class. In fact, he looked noticeably sad. All we got was a blank stare, which was so strange that our social mumblings were soon overtaken by sudden quietness. Even after we settled into our chairs and gave him our full attention, he said nothing for a few long minutes.

Finally, he shifted, arose from the edge of his desk, and started to walk slowly down the aisles between our desks. Stopping next to one student, he looked at him and said, "You." Again, he began walking. None of us had a clue about what was going on, so you could sense the uneasiness in the room.

"No way I'm making eye contact with this teacher," I thought.

He was close to the back of the classroom now, and I was too afraid to turn around. "And, you," he said, "come this way." Whew! He only summoned two students to follow him and led them to the front of the room where there was a small table with a chessboard set up on it along with two chairs. "Have a seat," he said. Both students looked very puzzled (as did the rest of us) and sat facing each other on opposite sides of the table. He asked them if they knew how to play chess and after they said, "Yes," he began to explain:

"My name is Professor Sol Weisman. This class is all about wisdom and is intended to teach you everything you need to know about how to minimize your shortcomings, while turning your failures into successes. Everyone except for the two students at the chessboard are to pay close attention to this video clip that I'm about to show you. It's the story about a man named Solomon. He was the nation of Israel's 3rd king whose rule followed that of his father, King David. King Solomon was considered the wisest man who had ever lived, but before his reign ended, he went from being a Man of Wisdom to a Man of Foolishness. His tale can be found in 1 Kings chapter one, but the highlights of his story pick up from the 3rd chapter and run through chapter 11. Watch, listen, and learn."

The professor dimmed the lights, instructed the two students to begin playing chess, and started the video.

We observed a young king to whom God appeared in a dream and asked him to make his desires known. At his young age, King Solomon asked for the ability to discern between good and evil so that he could be worthy to judge the great nation that God had placed in his care. In other words, his wish was to be endowed with wisdom above anything else. The Lord was so pleased with his request that He not only blessed him with a heart of wisdom, but he added the things that he didn't ask for: wealth and honor. He also promised him long life if he—like his father—walked in God's ways and kept His statutes and commandments. The narrator of the video described in detail the extent of Solomon's wealth and explained that his annual earnings in gold alone would be today's equivalent of 58 million dollars! That statement drew a gasp from all students in the room, including the two chess players.

At that moment, the professor instructed the players to redirect their attention to the game. When we learned about how vast the region was that he ruled, the chessmen once again shifted their eyes to the screen. It's getting crazy up in here! Finally, the mention of the King's 700 wives and his 300 concubines triggered such a boisterous ovation, that Professor Weisman stopped the video, turned on the lights, and ordered the chess players to return to their seats.

A hush fell over the room as the Professor returned to sit on the corner of his desk. Once again, no words were spoken for a couple of minutes.

With a strained whisper and a seemingly injured tone he said,

> *"That was me. No, my level of success wasn't even close to a speck on the radar, but yes, that was a glimpse of my life. It's not that I sought after fame, but fortune, women, and revelry were my idols. King Solomon started out on the right track by asking for wisdom over everything else. And then, countless wealth and great power guided his foot onto slippery ground and he fell into an arena of misdirected allegiance. In his heart the God of his father was*

replaced by the gods of his women. He went from building God's Temple to building pagan worship sites where even firstborn babies were burned alive as a sacrifice to fictitious deities. How did things get so twisted? Let's look at it from a practical perspective...

When I seated these two students and had them play a game of chess, their objective was to consider carefully each strategic move and anticipate an outcome. Their thought process should have been along the lines of, "If I decide on this choice, what possible consequence might it bring about?" Professor Sol continued with, "Did you notice how distracted they became when overhearing the narrator mention the King's wealth and power?" Furthermore, there was total disengagement from the chessboard when they heard how many women Solomon had. The Scriptures don't record the exact number of children there were as the result of so many women, but suffice it to say that there was an innumerous slew of kids who grew up without a father's undivided attention, love, or guidance. The enemy of the King's soul had lured him with fleeting pleasures and entrapped him by his own lusts. And, there you have it...checkmate!"

Interestingly, Solomon wrote the book of Proverbs. In Proverbs he admonishes us fervently to seek and embrace God's wisdom and to avoid people, places, and things that will obstruct our focus on the Lord. He writes of his foolishness but testifies of his return to a right relationship with God through repentance. Professor Weisman's demise bore an uncanny resemblance to King Solomon's. That's why he appeared as a stoic man who had been drained by his consequences. He shared with us how he hadn't seen his children in years because he left the family when they needed him most, and he wallows in regret because although he has reached out and tried to apologize and atone for his mistakes, they have no desire to see or talk with him. So sad. Moreover, this is so common throughout our culture.

The bell for our last class of the day rang and with hearts of ponderance, we all walked out. Although it saddened me to know the hurt within that man, I was excited about striving to exercise wisdom in all actions and decisions going forward. Professor Weisman's lecture and creative demonstration was brilliant. His delivery was powerful and his fervor unmatchable. Despite all that, he was a lonely, remorseful man, and I felt so much compassion for him. If he was so broken from his separation from his children over the years, I can only imagine how they felt during his earlier absence.

Situations like this take me back to my original promise to God. Put me in the game, Lord. I can't wait to become a father and love on my wife and kids. Nothing would be able to distract me from my obligation to serve them in a way that would make our home a place where we all looked forward to living with each other while building lasting memories. Experiencing the void from a child's perspective and witnessing it through the sufferings of men like King Solomon and Professor Weisman brought sufficiency to my self-assurance of becoming the best family man that I could possibly be. The knowledge that I acquired from that session suddenly made wisdom both a gift and a goal for me.

James 1:5-6 advises us to ask for wisdom and not doubt that God will grant us to receive it. However, King Solomon's mistake is that he traded the pleasure of God's fellowship for the pleasures of the world. I will go forward with a determination not to chase the shiny stuff and be the best child of God that I can be, so that I can be the best **dad** that I can be. He gave His Word (John 3:16); now I'm giving Him **my** word!

School is Out

...And real life is in! The return bus ride was better than the one to the school because it was without the anxiety. It had been a remarkable day of absorbing life-changing information. My job was now to delve into those biblical principles I avoided in the past and to reconfigure according to the wiser and healthier choices within my grasp. **THUMP**...*The bus rolled over a pothole and broke my train of thought. Now that I think of it, maybe it was a message and not an interruption. Perhaps it was just a reminder that despite all attempts to live right, there will be unexpected bumps in the road and uninvited challenges that will test my faith. Better yet, I suppose it was my first opportunity to take my new wisdom tool out of the box and put into practice the kind of reasoning that expands the borders of my thinking. Yeah, let's go with that!*

I'm back in my apartment complex now. The long day is behind me and all the comforts of home await. That included a soothing shower and some ice cream. Funny, I just realized that there was no lunch break today and I haven't had any real food. And yet, I'm not hungry! Very strange. I was gonna have some ice cream anyway. When I opened the freezer all that was in there was a bowl of onion rings with whipped cream on top. What!!! I didn't have any onion rings when I left, and I certainly wouldn't have put whipped cream on them if I did! This is not only weird, but also scary! I took a slow, confused walk into the living room and sat down on a sofa filled with water that swished all around my frame as I sat.

I must get out of here! This isn't my apartment!!! I ran to the front door and when I opened it there was a group of Christmas Carolers singing the National Anthem! I slammed the door and backpedaled into the apartment convinced that I was having some sort of breakdown. I laid on the floor and felt something crawling on my skin. I'm itching all over and with every frantic scratch I felt some sort of fluid beginning to cover me.

***

Squirming, yelling, grabbing at the air until...I woke up in a bed with chocolate chip cookies and an overturned glass of milk. I had fallen asleep watching TV with my late-night snack smeared all over me and my bed! After a matter of a few seconds, it dawned on me that my day at school was a dream!!!

This fictitious narrative is my way of bringing to light the non-fictional experience of my transformation. My "world" was dark, musty, and infested with ambiguities. There was no escape from it other than through the **"Door"** of Jesus Christ (John 10:7). I didn't become religious. That never earned a person anything but a ticket to legalism.

Rather, I became a prayer answered. The prayers of my mom's, my own, my friends interceding for me, who knows? All I know for sure is that on January 1, 1984, I became a "new creation" and the murky lens I used to look through became crystal clear. The "now what's" of my yesteryears didn't plague me like they used to do. That's because I accepted my role as a cast member in God's universal stage production, and I started to follow a script that is instructing, inspiring, and encouraging me continuously to press through tough times instead of cowering down as I used to do.

It's still hard sometimes to fall asleep on an empty stomach. But I never go to bed hungry as the "Bread of Life" never fails to satisfy my cravings!

8

Good Grief

Being a self-certified etymologist can be very demanding and more time consuming than I'd care for it to be. With interesting words, catch-phrases, and naming conventions frequently coming my way during conversations, it's hard for me to not consider or research their origin. For example: why do we yell, "Heads up!" when we really mean for a person to duck?

Why does a person sometimes say, "I have a terrific headache"? Would that suggest that they're enjoying it? Is the person who takes your order when dining at a restaurant really a "waiter"?

Think about it- aren't **we** the ones who are waiting for them to bring the food? How about "**Good**bye"? Sure, it's good to part ways when it happens to be someone you may not like very much. However, when "parting is such sweet sorrow," it's <u>not</u> a **good** bye. Hold on a minute, here we go again. "Sweet sorrow." How's that for an oxymoron? (I told you I had it bad!)

That leads us to wonder…what's the deal with "Good Grief"? When the "Peanuts" character Charlie Brown says it, it's light-hearted and playful. But from the realm of a realistic, humanistic world, most often it makes little sense to think that any good comes from grief. Then again, sometimes it does.

The extent or degree of grief we suffer varies according to a person's level of tolerance; the value placed on that which has been lost, the longevity of suffering, a substitutionary offset for what was lost, etc. What might this have to do with the overall theme of absent fathers? The pain associated with missing out on their presence or involvement is a grief that is heavy and requires healing. This chapter attempts to demonstrate how we can acknowledge our miseries courageously, allow for healthy grieving, and then find whatever good God might help us to recognize amid or after the suffering. Stepping in and out of progressive time zones, let's go...

Job

This man is quite a familiar figure from the Bible's Old Testament. Job was blessed with a wife and 10 children, an abundance of wealth in the form of livestock, and a large household, complete with servants. This was a dad who even made it a regular routine to rise early in the morning to offer sacrifices to God on his children's behalf - just in case they sinned against Him. He was also considered to be upright and blameless before God, which angered the devil. The Lord was so pleased with Job that He boasted of his faithfulness in a conversation with Satan, who argued that the only reason that Job was faithful was because of God's hedge of protection around him. With that, He gave the evil one permission to test Job's faith.

To give a brief overview of the story's elements, God allowed Satan to attack and destroy Job's livestock, children, servants, and affect his health. He was forbidden from taking his life, though, which would seem like the easy way out for a man who had been stripped of everything and everyone except his wife. Job had his weak moments, but he never gave in to cursing God for all that had happened to him. In the end, The Lord brought him physical healing, 10 more children, and doubled his livestock. No one can be sure why God would allow Job to be subjected to such a severe degree of suffering, but one thing we're certain about is that God—as in the account with Joseph in Egypt—turned grief into something good and recorded a lesson for us to learn thousands of years later.

The key points to extract from this story include a noble man worthy of God's adoration; a devoted dad who interceded for his children and covered them in prayer, a man who worshipped God despite his grief, and a servant of the Lord who refused to blame or curse God-even when things got a lot tougher than any of us could imagine. No, the grief was far from anything **good**, but God's providential plan refurbished Job's life and restored him to the fullness of his days. (Scriptural Reference: The Book of Job)

Sorrows Like Sea Billows

In1870, a man named Horatio Spafford became a senior partner in a large and profitable law firm in Chicago, Illinois. In addition to that, he was a successful real estate investor, a husband and father of four daughters and one son, and an elder in a Presbyterian church. Horatio was a wealthy, God-fearing man, with a family. (Sounds almost exactly like Job, doesn't he?)

For a while, life couldn't have been much better. However, it did become much worse, and grief struck with a violent force. That same year his four-year old son died of Scarlet Fever. On October 8th, 1871, the infamous Chicago Fire ravaged the city and left 300 people dead, 100,000 others homeless, and over 200 million dollars' worth of property was destroyed, including Mr. Spafford's real estate investments and law firm. He not only suffered great financial losses from the fire but hadn't yet recovered from the heartbreaking grief of his son's death.

Two years after the devastation he decided that the family needed a vacation to aid in the healing process. The plan was to sail to England to visit his friend and evangelist D.L. Moody who was there for a preaching engagement. At the last minute he was detained due to a business commitment, so he sent his wife and four daughters (ages 11, 9, 5, and 2) ahead and planned to meet up with them later. Tragically, their ship collided with an iron vessel and sank, killing 226 people including all four daughters. His wife miraculously survived and wired him from South Wales informing him of their catastrophic loss. Her telegram had just two words: "Saved alone." At this point my imagination is incapable of stretching far enough to capture the extent of this disaster, and perhaps yours can't either.

With the immensity of his grief, Mr. Spafford boarded a ship as soon as he could to join his wife overseas. While sailing close to the area where the family's ship sank, the captain called him to the bridge in observance of the tragic site.

Afterward, Mr. Spafford returned below to his berth and penned the lyrics to the hymn that many of us have sang during church services over the years. The musical score would then be written by a young man named Phillip Bliss. How's that for irony? A songwriter named Bliss, amid an episode that was anything but that. "It Is Well with My Soul" may not act as a reminder of what happened to the Spafford family, but it sure makes a difficult attempt to help us keep our focus on a Good God Who is still omnipresent amid excruciating grief.

Again, not **good** grief, but we'll keep trying. Don't put those tissues away yet – The Spaffords would go on to have three more children of which included another only son (Horatio) who was named after his deceased brother. He, too, died at the age of four years old. [3]

"Good" Friday

Now we enter a whole new tumbler of mixed emotions. Good Friday is observed every year two days before Resurrection Sunday (also known as Easter). Some churches have a special service in remembrance of the day that Jesus sacrificed His life for the sin of the world, while some families gather quietly at home to reflect on the event. Several business establishments and government offices are usually closed, and many employees are off. Sadly, there are entirely too many people who consider it Good Friday only because it's a paid holiday.

If they only knew...

Those who truly understand the depth of His crucifixion which involved betrayal by one of His disciples, a torturous beating, being spit on, mocked, and humiliated, find it extremely hard to consider it a "Good" Friday. We know that in His love it was all for the sake of mankind, but man was anything but kind to Him that day. He wasn't put to death using a humane method like lethal injection. Instead, He suffered a pain so excruciating that most of us turn away from watching when we see it depicted graphically on the TV or movie screen. Even still, the Divine nature in Him cried out, "Father, forgive them, for they know not what they do." Luke 23:34 (KJV)

Who says that? I guess Good Friday is a euphemism for Dark and Depressing Friday. Yeah, we labor against calling it "good" even though we understand why it is. If I had it my way, it would be renamed "Sacrificial Friday" and the day in which He was resurrected would be referred to as "Good Sunday!"

The whole point of the matter is that immeasurable **grief** belongs to that day of ultimate significance above all others in history, but so does indescribable **good**. Jesus conquered death and ushered us into the dispensation of grace, thereby making a way for us to receive everlasting life if we would only believe in Him. Here's praying that John 3:16 would carry a whole new meaning for some who may have been just using that verse of Scripture as a verbal knick-knack.

Dad's Passing Away

Separation Anxiety is a disorder that commonly afflicts children. The very thought of being apart from their parent(s) is enough to throw them off-kilter. Of course, I went through some of that as a child, but as I got older most of my longings trickled into a quiet pond of forgetfulness. We'll be putting a lid on this grievous chapter shortly and will explain how this all pertains to dads, but first we must cover a little more ground. For those of us who are "seasoned" enough to remember Gilbert O'Sullivan's 1971 song "Alone Again, (Naturally)," it will be easy to recognize a few modified lines from his ballad as they're interspersed within the last portions of this dreadful chapter. I promise a happier ending, but a stroll down this tender lane is all *"in an attempt to emphasize how it feels to be so sensitively shattered."*

My dad's world was shaken by several life-changing events that altered his norms and left him in unfamiliar surroundings. After falling down a flight of stairs, he suffered a blow to the head that required brain surgery to save him. He survived, but instead of his speech and motor skills being impaired (as the doctors thought they would be) his memory and personality were noticeably different.

Whereas he used to just kind of follow along with the program that his wife laid out for him, he became a bit more assertive and not as agreeable with her as he had always been. She and her friends still drank around him, but he had been given strict doctors' orders to give up alcohol since it would be dangerous to continue his drinking habits while on the medication that he was taking to prevent seizures. He was living in a place where liquor consumption was frequent, but he couldn't participate any longer. That was a tough one!

For the first time in many years his relationship with his wife took a radical turn, and it appeared as though the walls were closing in on him. About a year later, one of his wife's drinking buddies took sick and passed away. The remaining two friends buried her and resumed their activities. Six months after that, the last friend died suddenly, leaving my dad's wife as the last one standing. The two friends occupied the same plot, until dad's wife also expired a few months later. So, all three died in the same year and were buried together in the same burial space. Dad was now alone.

Because the apartment they lived in was now too big for a lone occupant, he was forced to downsize. One might think that resetting at 63 years old isn't such a bad thing, but in his case it was probably hard. After all, his lifestyle was customary and his affiliations were typical, thus making every effort to reform that much more challenging—especially when he had to give up drinking. He still had some neighborhood friends of his own who did not take his dire warning to abstain seriously, tempting and coercing him every chance they got. That elevator would take them up to his 11th floor apartment or take him down to the sitting area to meet up with them in front of his building. Either way, they'd meet, they'd drink, they'd leave, and he'd be left, *"Alone Again (Naturally)."*

My sister, Denise, would see him more often than I would because she lived very close to him. She became his company and primary caregiver, but one day I made it a point to drop by. That visit was like no other time spent ever before. Not only was he sober, but he was in an upbeat mood. I don't recall everything we spoke about, but I do remember feeling compelled to talk to him about the Lord and he was very receptive.

Before leaving, I prayed with him, which was an all-time first! When we finished, he walked me to the elevator, and I waited before getting on just so I could see him walk down the hall and go into his apartment. He turned and looked at me from a distance, did this little funny head-bob motion to make me laugh, then went in. That would be the last time I'd see him alive.

It was no more than a couple of weeks after my special time with him when my phone rang, and Denise told me to come to his apartment. She had been trying to reach him for two days without any response, and had just found him deceased in his bedroom. When I arrived on that hot August afternoon there was an unnatural stillness in the air. I sat with Denise and my 5-year-old nephew, Carlton, with him not fully understanding what was going on, while the two of us circumvented the reality of dad's permanent departure.

My time to confront my emotions came after I returned home and eased my way into a secluded space. No, I didn't grow up with dad nor was he actively involved in my life, but *"I remember I cried when my father died never trying to hide the tears."* Of course, I couldn't say that my grief was attributed to many good times we enjoyed together. Rather, I ached over our not being able to bond with each other. And now he's gone for good...or, maybe not. I was reminded of that last visit with him and how we talked about God and how he joined me in prayer.

Perhaps that was all he needed to open the door of his heart and let Jesus in. If so, what a day it will be when we meet either in that new heaven or new earth! It would be so heartwarming to hear his sober voice call me "son," which I've waited an earthly lifetime to hear, and to finally get that hug from a dad who is home to stay. That would be well worth all the agony from years gone by. God can bring some good out of all that grief and give us a fresh beginning. What a glorious day that would be!

Mom's Passing Through

Yesterday evening's weather outburst came through as a fast and furious intruder without even a hint of its approach. One minute the sky was partly cloudy with a peaceful air—your proverbial calm before the storm. Next came the ultra-dark, ominous clouds like the ones from the scene in the Ten Commandments movie where God is about to part the Red Sea. Finally, a tornado came, and severe thunderstorm warnings were all over the TV – followed by raging winds, torrential rain, and power outages. The onslaught lasted for about 30 minutes and just like before it started, a return to calmness. Life can be like that. Smooth beginnings, turbulent episodes along the way, and an ease into peacefulness on the back end. Such is how it was with mom's life.

I consider it a blessing to be able to reach far back into my memory bank to that afternoon when mom picked me up from my crib after my nap, held me in her arms, and called me by a nickname that she obviously made up in the moment. (I'll just keep that one to myself.)

For me and my sister, those were the calm days long before the storms of life came along. But, for mom, her winds were swirling, although we were oblivious to it. It would be only a few short years later when things began to get rough for her. That's when she'd end up wearing an apron and "pants" at the same time. She became both mom and dad, giving us the security and necessities that we were unable to provide for ourselves. Her love was gentle at times and firm when it needed to be. Her humor was zany (which is where I get it from), yet she was not amused when we tried her.

She didn't remarry after her breakup with dad, so—in the natural—she raised us singlehandedly. In the supernatural, it was none other than the Spirit of the Lord that carried her as she carried us. The awareness of where her strength came from led to her accepting Jesus Christ as Lord 25 years before she died.

Little did we know it would be a storybook sendoff. My sister and I held a surprise party two days before mom's 80th birthday. The festivities included friends and relatives (some of whom she hadn't seen in many years), one of her favorite singers, guest speakers who honored her for the memories they shared, and a musical slideshow that my sister and I put together as an audio/visual "thank you" for all she'd done for us throughout the years. It was a beautiful event, but we had no idea that it would turn out to be a farewell tribute. A couple days after the party she got sick and had to be rushed to the emergency room. Two months later she passed on. The party was certainly a pleasant surprise for her, but the way in which she left this earth was not a surprise to us.

That Sunday evening, I arrived at the hospital having come straight from work. By now she was in Hospice care. I spoke with her the night before and told her I was coming for a visit, but God's Divine providence had planned otherwise. When I stepped off the elevator and headed toward her room, there were a few fast-moving attendants in front of her door. One of them spotted me heading their way and intercepted me before I made it to the room. She told me that they were getting mom ready for bed and asked me to have a seat in the waiting area until she came to get me.

Twenty minutes later she came for me with a smile on her face and walked me to the room. With her smile and her telling me that she was just talking with my mom a little while ago led me to believe that she had enjoyed one of mom's typically humorous conversations. That prompted me to smile also until she opened the door for me to see a couple of nurses standing by her bed looking expressionless. It didn't take long for my smile to disappear as they all just kind of looked at me in anticipation of a response.

"Is she gone?" I asked. One of them said, "Yes".

Perhaps it was shock, but there was no crying in my immediate repertoire. When the nurse explained to me that she had been servicing hospice patients for over 20 years and that this was only the 2nd time she saw someone leave so peacefully, I understood why she approached me smiling. That was truly a perfect example of "good" grief. Mom's **"storm"** passed away, not her. Her role as single parent playing a dual role had come to an end, and now it was time for that blessed assurance she was promised. She ran a good race and made it to the finish line where the Lord was waiting to take her to her **real** home, and I was so thankful that she was spared from pain and discomfort.

When the doctor arrived for the official declaration, he positioned his stethoscope in a few places before looking at me and shaking his head, "No." If I had thought to, I would have asked him to place it on **my** chest at which time I would have nodded "Yes." Medical studies declare that after 18 weeks in the womb a baby can hear its mother's heartbeat. That makes perfect sense to me. I probably felt mom's heartbeat before I even heard it! In fact (figuratively speaking), I still feel it! No doubt it's due to the strong "Wi-Fi" connection we established during the gestation phase.

After calling Denise and sharing the news, she made it to the room rather quickly. That moment broke my heart. She was the one who always kept her emotions in check, but not this time. The sands of time were in reverse, and she became the same little girl whose tears drenched her pillow in the aftermath of a traumatic disappointment. We recovered, planned her homegoing, and got through it by God's continued grace.

On my way home from the service, I made the mistake of driving alone. Precious memories didn't delay until I made it to my apartment. Instead, they pulled me into a trance while waiting for a traffic light to turn green. The motorist behind me, unaware of my pensive state, became outraged when I didn't advance quickly enough after the light changed. He leaned on his horn and added an unpleasant (to say the least) hand gesture to ensure that I felt his disgust. I'd like to think that if he only knew where I was just coming from, he would have been filled with more compassion than anger.

Saying farewell to dad was heartbreaking because of all that we missed out on, and it left me hoping that he made peace with God and invited Christ to be his Lord and Savior. With mom, the sadness of missing her presence is superseded by my confidence in knowing that our reunion is guaranteed because of the covenant we have with the One Whose sacrifice on the cross paved the way for us to enjoy eternal life as it was intended originally. In both cases, I am thankful that God used them as earthly vessels to bring forth my being. And, if His will allows, I only ask that He let them know that I miss them both and rejoice at the very thought of seeing them once again, but this time in paradise.

A Shattered Dream

The Prophet Jeremiah is referred to as "The Weeping Prophet." He is the author of five chapters that are displayed poetically in the biblical book of Lamentations. His outpouring of grief is due to the anguish he felt over the capture and destruction of Jerusalem by the Babylonians. Although his free verse style of expressing his pain can be a challenge to understand, one can easily become infused with his inward suffering while reading through his writings. Consider this poem as an example of emotional agony:

***

Should I dare ask to tap the pulse of normality?

God forbid.

And when He did, my heart would bleed beyond a pause.

A cause wherein each sacrifice is undefined.

Even the kindest words are as weapons

impaling a battered soul until a niche cries out.

May it be unoccupied;

tolerant;

embossed by the audible calm of nature's symphony.

The seasoned chord of a breeze shall begin to knead,

while waters saturate and purge.

Sing, the anointed gaggle of songbirds!

Theirs is the fifth day,

the seventh, mine.

Benign, a tainted core may rest in the Alpha,

but may the Omega place hope within my reach.

'til all who love as I encircle Thee...

might I endure.

***

Can you feel it?

No, it wasn't written by Jeremiah. It was written by a middle-aged man 29 years ago who submitted it as an entry for a poetry writing contest. As the story is told, after church service one Fathers' Day, his grief over that national observance drove him to an isolated spot at home where he penned his frustrations in a form so abstract that no one except him would be able to detect his suffering. The poem was accepted and printed in an anthology titled "Seasons to Come" published by The National Library of Poetry in 1995. It turns out that while he was sharing his accomplishment with coworkers, one person in particular—the director of human resources—pulled him aside and asked (with concern) for an explanation of the sorrow camouflaged within the words.

The author of the poem knew he was "busted" on the spot, so he came clean. He confessed that he wrote the poem thinking it would be a release for him. He further explained that Fathers' Day celebrations were very painful for him because he couldn't enjoy them from either end of the spectrum. Not only did he grow up without his father being in the home or actively involved in his life, but also, he was unable to become a father due to circumstances too distressing to reveal. So, he wrote the poem after learning about various artists who often used their craft to relieve themselves of pent-up sentiments. With that enlightenment, the coworker expressed empathy and offered the best words of encouragement she was able to convey.

In case your suspicions haven't kicked in yet, the author of the poem was me.

That's right, the same one who as a little fellow prayed a vow to God that when I became a man, I was going to be a loving, devoted father and be all to my children what I didn't have myself. I stood ready to keep that promise for many years, but the Lord had a different plan for me. Part of my calling serves a dual purpose. Not only am I to be a herald to those who have been wounded deeply by the absence of a dad in their lives, but also to those among what seems to be a minority of men whose desire to become a dad hasn't been fulfilled.

Unfortunately, not many who have experienced either (or both) even consider it to be a blessing, nor do they empathize with men who populate this grievous zone. That is most likely because there isn't much value placed on the privilege of seeing a child run to them with open arms when they arrive home. Hearing an excited son or daughter call them "Daddy" has become stale and routine, while some of us have never turned around to see if we were being addressed.

Of course, we live in an imperfect world and not all dads get to have a son who will continue the bloodline and pass along the family name. Some may never even walk a daughter down the aisle. But there is something very special about feeling as though you're a part of the circle of life. How do I know? Because I've seen it in the eyes and on the faces of family members, friends, coworkers, neighbors, and strangers when their turn comes to gaze through that maternity window in awe. For the rest of us, the constant reminders are relentless, surrounding, and painful. And by the way, here's two things not to say to a person who is unable to experience the blessing of seeing his child born: "You're better off" and, "You want mine?" Not funny, and not compassionate!

Despite this being a double-whammy and a tragic shattered dream, there is some good to come out of this grief. It is from an uncanny inkling that someday it will mean something so significant that the joy in store will by far outweigh the agony. I often think about the miracle that Jesus performed when He fed more than 5,000 people with two fish and five loaves of bread. For that event to have been recorded in all four gospels (Matthew, Mark, Luke and John) strongly hints of a noteworthy message for subsequent multitudes throughout the ages.

Could it be a metaphorical lesson about brokenness? As I sat in church one day, my spirit was on the edge of its seat as a pastor exposed what could be seen as a deeper meaning behind God's miracle. First, Jesus took the loaves of bread and gave thanks to the Father for His provision. Then, He distributed it to the masses. Okay, so how might that apply to my shattered dream of becoming a dad? The loaves of bread, while in a singular configuration, would only have been able to feed five people. However, as they were distributed in a broken, fragmented consistency, they were then capable of blessing thousands.

Lord, I think I got it!

Give God **thanks** for the provision of the "Bread of Life" and for that sincere desire I had to father my own children, and to love them the way I wanted my father to love me. But through the **brokenness** of my disappointment, I am now able to extend way beyond my dream and "feed" Your love to multitudes. If I had been blessed to become a biological dad, I probably would have intensified my portions of adoration toward them so much that it might have bordered on idolatry. Instead, boundless love can be dispersed and have much more of an impact than love that is limited to my offspring alone.

The Savior of my soul is the giver of life - abundant life, that comes with the happiest new beginnings that will last for all eternity. The key is to focus on the haves and not on the have-nots. Adam and Eve made the mistake of not doing that. Theirs was a garden full of trees bearing delicious fruit to enjoy. God placed a restriction on only one tree of the many and commanded them to not eat from it. They lusted after the "have-not" instead of appreciating "the haves," and the rest is history.

I am not completely out of the woods, but the lesson I learned that day about how God can use my brokenness to bless others helps me cope much better than I used to, and I am believing that one day my healing will be complete and removed from my archives.

Yes, grief covers an immeasurably wide range of assorted calamities. Paternal neglect, abuse, and abandonment should not be one of them. Any one of those misdoings are sure to leave irreparable scars on a child that can carry over into adulthood and cast shadows of destruction in their path. Dads must strive to be part of the solution rather than the problem. Consider it an honor to be able to optimize your role as your child's hero and agent for the Lord's biological bounty.

The grief that tormented Jeremiah because of the destruction of Jerusalem will be replaced with indescribable joy when the new Jerusalem is brought forth. The grief that was meant to be Joseph's demise was turned into his delight instead, as God showered him with protection and favor. As for the archetype of grief, look at the blood-stained cross that Jesus used to give us that "Good Friday," the day that His suffering meant that ours would only be for a short time in the full scope of eternity. It was the love of a Father, the trust of

His Son, and the ultimate exhibit of the kind of relationship that is a wonder to behold, even on an earthly level.

9

2020 Vision

When Denise called me on the evening of January 10th, 2020, little did she know that we had been playing a different type of phone tag over the years. It was the kind where we'd take turns phoning each other to announce shocking news. Hers to me was when dad died, mine to her was when mom died. This time, she started the conversation without a greeting, just straight to the point.

"Are you sitting down?" she asked.

I didn't brace myself for disturbing news because her somewhat up-beat tone tipped me off that she was calling to deliver some pleasant information. I sat down, and then she served me a whopper. Our long-lost sister and brother (whom we had never met or spoken with) found us after 64 years through the help of a well-known online ancestry service. That ranked high among the most shocking news I had ever received! For decades we knew that they were out there somewhere and thought about them often, but neither of us tried to find them for concern that the time just wasn't right. Okay, into the "Time Machine" we go for clarity regarding the full essence of this portion of my passage.

Dad's departure from our home wasn't only due to his and mom's inability to coexist. Apparently he was involved in sharing himself with a love interest beyond the bounds of holy matrimony. (How's that for a soft euphemism?) As a result, Cheryl and Charles were born and became distant siblings until Cheryl's daughter (Leah) gifted her mom by launching an extensive search to connect with us. Way to go, Leah!

Denise and I were curious about them throughout the years and even had their baby picture in our possession, which was given to us by our mother. Yep, **our** mother! In case you're scratching your head right now trying to make sense of that, let me help you out. The pieces of this puzzle were put together for me when I became a young teenager. Remember that summer evening when as a nine-year-old I heard mom crying in the next room? Well, apparently, she had received a letter informing her of dad's other two children along with a photo of them. This is where I applaud her for having aberrant restraint under weepy duress. Not only did she not dispose of the photo, but she kept it and gave it to us years later while explaining that we had a sister and brother out there. I'm so glad she did!

The wavy screen of retrospect returns us to 2020 where Denise and I were exchanging dubious chatter over the phone. How do we process this news-breaking info? How do we proceed with it? Or should we? Since the connection was made between Leah and one of our 2nd cousins, should we just let them communicate while we lurk behind the scenes and decide at what point (if any) we come forward and reveal ourselves? It didn't take me long to volunteer for frontline duty. Denise retrieved Cheryl's phone number from our cousin, passed it along to me, and I texted her two days later.

The January 12, 2020, text conversation went like this:

> **Me:** *Just checking. Is this Cheryl?*
> **Cheryl:** *Yes. Sorry, this number is not saved in my phone. Who is this?*
> **Me:** *Hi Cheryl. I am struggling with how to put my words together right now. Please have a seat. My name is Rick.*

Formal name, Richard Rogers. Yes, I am your brother.
Cheryl: *Praise the Lord! To have a family is a blessing. To know that you want to talk to me...I feel more blessed!*

We had our very first voice-to-voice phone conversation 15 minutes later, and it was incredible! Her being five years younger than me (with Charles being 7 years younger) meant that I was no longer the "baby" of the family. Not sure what kind of perks came with that, but it didn't matter. Denise and I had new siblings, and the links were no longer missing! The next day I received a text message from the hero of the story. Leah was an overnight sensation of a niece who took bold steps to bring us together.

Here's how it went:

Leah: *Good afternoon, my name is Leah. I am Cheryl's 2nd daughter. She gave me your number. I am not trying to bother you in any way, but I just wanted to thank you for reaching out to my mom. Unlike my father's family, on my mother's side it was pretty much just the four of them. Now three are living, but she said she always wished she had other siblings and a bigger family.*
Me: *Hi Leah. Are you kidding me? You are no bother at all. In fact, you're my hero!!! I am ecstatic about meeting my sister after all these years, and look forward to meeting my brother as well. As for you, my niece, have a super-blessed day, and be sure that we will all meet soon!*
Leah: *The excitement and nervousness on her face made my day yesterday. I look forward to meeting you, your wife, and anyone else who wishes to meet us also. Please save my number (my mom is not the best with hers) and you can contact me anytime. Most people do when they're looking for her, lol. Have a blessed day, Uncle Rick!*

These dialogues set the stage for a grand first encounter with blood relatives that was too awesome to describe accurately. My wife and I flew up to Orange, New Jersey; Denise and my nephew drove from Bronx, New York, and my other new niece (Cheryl's oldest daughter) flew in from California. This appointment was so special, that it even fell on February 29th. Leah and her husband (Woody) hosted a dinner party in honor of the ultra-special occasion. When we walked in, it was enchanting!

There were lasting hugs, tears, laughter, and a video recording to capture the extraordinary moment that we had been anticipating for quite a long time. Seeing new nieces, nephews, great nieces and great nephews made up for lost time, and we had so much fun with pointing out the physical resemblances among us. The timing for our meeting couldn't have been more perfect as the surge of the Covid19 pandemic hit hard two weeks later and shut everything down. Had we not gotten together when we did, the suspense would have taunted us for who knows how long.

With understanding that stories of distant family members meeting for the first time don't always have a pleasant outcome made us appreciate it even more. As an additive, it turns out that the two sisters have lived within walking distance of each other for 15 years! Not only that, because of their involvement with the same chapter of the United Federation of Teachers, they've been in the same room during annual events and might have even met not knowing that they were sisters!

We all stay in touch, and what ices the cake is that last week, Cheryl, Leah, and family moved from New Jersey and are now living near my wife and me in North Carolina. That being the good part of it all now brings us to the not so good.

Four of a Kind

Denise and I couldn't boast of having a devoted father at home or actively immersed in our upbringing, but at least we knew him and spent some time with him. Cheryl and Charles were not able to say that since they had never met him. Because of that, they had many questions and looked to us to help satisfy their curiosities. We could have easily said that we saw the worst of things, while they felt badly about not seeing anything at all.

Collectively we share similar sentiments. To begin with, we all agree that the deficiency of a fatherly ingredient left us often confused and wondering why dad didn't want to be with us. As youngsters, we didn't understand the logistics of collapsed relationships and why it should victimize us. Our moms didn't abandon us, so why should dad? A reason for that is much more complicated than a juvenile mind can comprehend.

Without answers, we each had to whisper, scream, or cry into our own pillows. Another commonality is that none of us could say that we ever had a sober, meaningful conversation with him, nor were any of us recipients of his love or affection.

We laid claim to Charles as our "brother from another mother," and Cheryl as our "sister from the same mister."

Together we see a blessing from God—once again—making good out of something not intended to be good. Indeed, we have scars from what happened, but we're hopeful that our story (though not uncommon) will play a major part in provoking men to be more empathetic towards innocent kids left with splintered hearts due to their leaving. In addition, I will underscore the importance of this message penetrating the hearts and minds of any men out there who stand at the cusp of yielding to their sensualities without any regard for the possibility of damaging ramifications. If you've been victimized by the abandonment of a father, you might be a bit more receptive to this message and its appeal for you to stop the cycle.

Boy, oh Boy

When Charles and I compared notes, we found that some of the struggles we faced were somewhat similar. He grew up not knowing where his father was, while often I didn't know either. We were both surrounded by question marks that clouded our minds with mysteries about what would cause us to be left without a father.

As I listened to Charles' episodes, it saddened me to know that his curiosity was so severe and persistent, that his mom got tired of him asking about his dad. That led to her reaching a point where she couldn't tolerate it anymore and sent him off to live with his much older sister and her husband. He tells of how difficult it was for him to be under his brother-in-law's strict discipline, and how his mom suggested that he join the Army so they could "make a man" out of him.

It's funny how I enlisted in the Navy seeking the same outcome, although signing up was under my own volition. Although there was no way I'd have been able to fill in all the blanks for him, it was obvious that my sharing some fun facts with him brought a little comfort to his lifetime of despair. He and dad were both left-handed, both came equipped with a dry (but hilarious) sense of humor, and all three of us shared the same notable features: bald head, mustache, and dimples.

Whereas we might have benefited from sitting around talking for hours about how we dealt with the mutual hardship of life in a fatherless home, it didn't seem like a good idea since it would have stirred the pot and rekindled bad feelings. So, we engaged (and still engage) in small talk and we text frequently, keeping things shallow and light-hearted.

Daddy's Girls

Cheryl recently revealed to me that they were told that dad was deceased, which is why he wasn't around. From what I've heard, that was a common technique used as a way of staying in the safe place of not having to deal with persistent questions. Cheryl seemed to accept that explanation with a bit of sadness, but Charles' anguish didn't let up. Even Denise admits to being affected by our dad not being there, but in a recent talk with her she leaned more toward classifying her symptom as a subtle void rather than a haunting disturbance. She was always the one who didn't exactly wear her heart on her sleeve. Sometimes I wished I was more like her, but aside from what girls feel versus what boys feel, we were wired differently.

Even to this day sometimes I tease her about those Christmas mornings when I would be out under that tree opening my presents before the break of dawn. In between gifts I'd run to wake her up so she could come out and see what she got, but she'd just brush me off, roll over, and go back to sleep. Meanwhile, I was wound tight and bustin' at the seams! In all honesty, my uncontrollable enthusiasm started at the beginning of the month. She was just cool that way, which is how—on the exterior—she carried herself throughout her dad-less years.

Both Denise and Cheryl believe that they were at a disadvantage when it came to dating experiences and partnership choices. From what I've discovered, a lot of that has to do with a few different factors:

- Trust and commitment issues stemming from what they witnessed in dad's relationships.

- A nagging hunch that abandonment is inevitable.

- Not having a good example of a successful marriage to follow.

****Dads: These are only some of the residual effects that girls suffer if you forsake the importance of helping them with their developmental stages of becoming a young woman. When you underestimate **your** value, they underestimate **theirs**.*

At this point I thought it would be a good idea to check with a couple of other ladies who are special friends rather than family members. They **are** both like family, just not blood related. The particulars are somewhat different, but their heartaches are the same. One of them almost didn't survive the traumatic events that occurred in her life but thank God for His intervention and protection.

The first case involves another addition to our family. Cathy and I have "adopted" her as the daughter who just kind of snuck up on us from out of the blue. She is a very young woman who is well beyond her years in terms of intellect and maturity.

She has survived a home life in which her father was there for a while but might as well not have been. She tells of him being extremely neglectful and emotionally abusive at the same time. After middle school bullying, family hardships, and bad relationships finished with her, she fought a weak (but successful) battle against taking her own life and checking out for good. All her sufferings are attributable to the lack of a loving dad in the home.

Like so many other ladies, navigating through the gauntlet of toxic relationships is one of the lingering afflictions caused by her domestic ordeal. The good news is that she was able to enjoy what she describes as "the happiest times of my life" when her mom remarried a man who became her stepdad. Thank God for men who step up, rather than step out! Her past is behind her now, and she is promised a brighter future since she has accepted Jesus Christ as her Lord and Savior.

To lose her dad in a fatal car accident is a tragedy most of us can't imagine having to go through. That is what my friend, Tammy, had to endure. She was only two years old at the time, and although she was too young to understand or remember it all, it became a developing sorrow as she grew older and entered adulthood. She tells of often wondering what life would have been like with her dad and if he'd have been proud of her.

As a remote witness to the relationship that she shares with her stepfather, Charlie, and the love and pride that he has for her, it's easy to assume that her birth dad would have adored her. Challenges with selective dating weren't as pronounced as the other ladies because her stepdad **was** her dad! He was right there to do the screening for her and to provide the security that all young ladies need.

Unlike the others, her biological father didn't abandon her. Instead, his was a sad and accidental departure that paved the way for God to bless her with an "appointed" dad who was—and still is—ever-present in her life. She's cleared many hurdles to become successful in the "Here and Now" as the life of the party, a good companion to her devoted man, Tim, and the best dog-mom on the planet. My prayer is for her to believe that success in the **"There and Later"** rests on her trusting the One Who has seen her through a heartbreaking misfortune that no toddler should ever have to experience.

Times "Scare"

It was only two months into the new year and many of us were wishing we could push that Times Square Ball back up to the top and start over again. On a good note, Denise and I finally got to unite with a brother and sister we had lost hope of ever meeting, but that highlight would quickly be overshadowed by a barrage of bad tidings.

Our Pastor's wife's health began to decline again, leaving a congregation hopeful yet grief-stricken. We had unnatural, natural disasters so frequent and intense that words like "unprecedented," "epic proportions," and "infrequent" were common among their descriptions. And then the gut-punch...Covid 19. When it first started to spread and a few fatalities were reported, the social atmosphere was numbed by its newness and ability to disrupt our normal, everyday lives.

There were a lot of people walking around with that blank and worried look that said, "What is happening here?"

Stores and schools were closed temporarily, travel was halted, and a wide range of events were cancelled. Suddenly, it was "quiet."

You may be wondering what all of this has to do with fatherhood, but stay with me.

When I was a sailor serving on board that Navy Destroyer, my division's sleeping compartment was located at the rear bottom deck of the ship. Oddly, the deafening sound of the rudder and its mechanics became a sort of lullaby as we cruised through the vast seas and oceans during the night. On rare occasions we would lose engine power, bringing us to a complete stop in the water. This temporary silence had a reverse effect on our peaceful sleep, as we would be awakened by the eerie silence. Think of it...noise put us to sleep, silence woke us up.

As such, the broad effects of the pandemic temporarily woke us out of the "sleep" of yesterday's agitations and forced us into an uncertainty of what our tomorrows might bring. We became aware of our vulnerability and started worrying about casualties, food supplies, and the availability of medical attention. In those moments we were like young scouts who were frightened by a campfire story. The next, it was business as usual. Well, not exactly.

There were harsh lines drawn in the sand dividing folks between political parties, mask-wearing mandates, vaccine impositions, social distancing, and more. Unfortunately, the new "normal" seemed to display more scowls than smiles once the masks came off. Rules were compromised, signs were ignored (in more ways than one), and fewer people had that "What just happened here" look on their faces. Still, there were many who stepped into a new appreciation for the good things and were more conscious about not taking things—or relationships—for granted.

Yes, 2020 was a pivotal year, and the following one didn't offer much relief. But as we turned the corner on things, there was still evidence that a great number of people remember how important it is to have papa's hand to hold onto as he leads us through the labyrinth. Dads are needed now more than ever before. They need to be there to try their best to answer the tough questions and show their strength during tough times.

And even before he may become a husband and possibly a father, much good can come out of showing him how valued he is and worthy of support and encouragement. When it's time, he will be better equipped to stay the course and be the "Moses" of a family enslaved by decaying principles as he leads them to a place promised by a greater father than himself.

10

Wonders to Behold!

If you're a big fan of astonishments, prepare to be blown away! In order to experience the full effect of these mind-boggling phenomena you're going to need a few things to include in your setting:

- A secluded, quiet room (preferably with a window, but not necessary)

- Dim or no lighting if it's nighttime

- No external noises (if possible)

- Very soft, easy-listening music with no lyrics (optional)

- A comfortable chair

No worries, there's nothing spooky going on here. We're just creating a relaxed atmosphere that will allow for uninterrupted deep thought which will help you to think about your Dad in a way you may never have before. If you set the stage correctly and allow yourself to settle into the framework, you are guaranteed to end up with a totally different perspective than when this session began.

A Chosen Champion

And the winner is…YOU! You shot out of that starting gate at a "blazing" speed of about 28 miles per hour.[4] You were competing against nearly 100 million "contestants," [5] (really!) which meant that your chances of winning the race was pretty much zero to none! Still, you darted, dashed, and relentlessly maneuvered your way past the others while your offensive linemen blocked for you (not really) until you found a clearing among the masses and forged ahead with fierce determination. The "marathon" took only about 30-45 minutes, [6] but it was grueling as you headed for that finish line and was crowned the victor!

Your prize? An egg. One simple egg which you found comfort in fertilizing.

Once there, your real journey began.

This is your first, "think about it." You were selected by God Himself to win that race and become the formation of a live being. The very first man He created didn't have to compete against hundreds of millions of others vying for the prize. He just kind of chilled in the dust of the earth and was formed from scratch by the hand of God. Due to that man's sin the rest of us had to work at everything. But that's okay because we won life, and mankind was given a second chance to get it right.

There are at least two truths to be learned from this.

First, **you** are a first! You were a champion even before entering your mother's womb.

Second, none of us should ever say, "I can't swim." God deemed you important enough to make room for you in His grand scheme of creation. He has a plan for your life and for all those who are born through you.

Understanding this should lay the groundwork for how you think of yourself.

Self-significance should not be contingent upon how we measure up against another person and their accomplishments or possessions, but rather on how precious we are to the One who made us.

> ***Dads: Many of you don't set out with the intent to walk away from your kids. Often, you've fallen for the delusion within yourself that it's **you** who are not important, therefore you're not important to your children and your absence from their life is not a big deal. No two things could be further from the truth. They need you, and God needs you to accept the assignment and complete the mission. Be the champion to them that you've already proven to be - even before you were born. The race is much different now and so is the prize. It's the reward of that impromptu, tender moment when you look into the eyes that say, "Thank you, dad. You've always been there for me."

Something for Every<u>body</u>

Next, let's look at some of the amazing components of your physical makeup. After going through the Germinal, Embryonic, and Fetal stages of development, you entered the world as a baby.[7] In most cases, you'll have over 650 different muscles,[8] about 206 bones,[9] and eyes with at least two million working parts.[10] Think that's mind-blowing? We're just getting started! That heart of yours which began beating about six weeks into the gestation period is the very first organ to form.

Perhaps that's because it provides the bodily rhythm needed for all other instruments to follow in order to make good "music." (Had to get a plug in for my bass guitar playing days.) Now that it's in place and operating, (on average) it's beating more than 108,000 times per **day.** At that rate, it's pumping about 83 gallons of blood an hour, which adds up to almost 2,000 gallons per day! [11]

Now, multiply 365 times the number of full years you've lived. Then, multiply that total times 2,000 and you'll have the **approximate** number of gallons of blood your heart has pumped since you were born!

It's okay to sit back and say, "Wow!" if you'd like, but wait...there's more!!

This planet we live on is huge, with its circumference measuring approximately 25,000 miles. Okay, here we go again, and I'm going to need a little help with this because here's where things cross over into the unfathomable. Medical science has determined that the blood being pumped by our heart travels through over 60,000 miles of arteries, veins, and capillaries. [12]

That said, if you were to lay those blood vessels end-to-end, they would **circle the globe more than twice!!!** I don't know about you, but I cannot imagine that! I'd even have trouble believing that they would reach the end of the block, much less around the earth two and a half times.

With the heart being the first major organ formed and understanding its prominence, consider the last major organ...the lungs. They are the perpetual airbags that deliver the oxygen we need to survive. Knowing that we inhale and exhale approximately 22,000 times daily, [13] maybe those lungs were last because after the body was complete it was time for the christening of God's breath to finish the project. In order to fully appreciate the gift of breath God gave us, we can follow the same formula we used to see how much blood we've pumped to determine how much air we've breathed in our lifetime.

Genesis 2:7 reminds us that God formed man from the dust of the ground and breathed the breath of life into him. Shortly after that He made woman, using one of the man's ribs. Those two beings were the only ones who weren't constructed after pre-existing biological dynamics. Instead, they were designed directly by the hands of the Heavenly Father Himself. That makes it easy to answer the question, "Which came first, the chicken or the egg?" Since God created everything in its completed form first, all creatures after that were subject to an intricate, systematic means of reproduction.

Before continuing with this journey, I find it necessary to offer the first of two formal apologies. Somehow, and if possible, I want my father to know that I am so sorry for placing too much of an expectation on him. The very young and immature mind in me blamed him for not having the courage and "stick-to-it-ive-ness" to live up to his responsibilities as the leader of our family.

Although his absence and non-involvement caused much pain and sorrow, I learned later that he suffered the same pain I did by not having a loving, devoted dad in his life either. It is not the rhythm-beating, blood-pumping heart that I speak from right now. Rather, it's the heart where the person of the Holy Spirit resides and intercedes on my behalf. My passionate hope is that before he passed away, he heard a knock on the chamber of his own heart and opened the door to receive Jesus as his Lord and Savior. In that, I would be extremely excited to see him, having no record of the past, and enjoying a future with no end. I'm so sorry, dad...so sorry.

Taking a break now...

In a Good Space

By now, we should not only understand how precious and meaningful we are to the One who created us, but having a recognition of Him as the Father of all fathers should be locked into place. If so, let's pick up where we left off and turn up the burners a bit. Romans 1:20

(NLT) states that *"...since the world was created, people have seen the earth and sky. Through everything God made, they can clearly see his invisible qualities—his eternal power and divine nature. So they have no excuse for not knowing God."*

That verse is enough to answer the question, "What about those who have never heard the gospel?" By observing His creation alone, they've seen it! That same power included the earth and the firmament, along with a moon, a sun, and other planets in our solar system. We'll just take a glimpse at that "small" portion of the universe since we won't be able to handle much else beyond that anyway. Our earth—as mentioned—is quite large. However, when we view it in a broader context, here goes...

It is estimated that 1,300,000 earths can fit into our sun. [14]

Just to spell it out for emphasis, that's **one million, three hundred thousand!** We can certainly assume that the sun is humungous despite it not appearing as such when we look at it in the sky, but I guess 93 million miles away lends to the illusion that it's not as large as it sounds.

Do you think that's far? Check this out: Voyager 2 is a spacecraft that was designed to study the edge of our solar system. It was launched on August 20, 1977. It crossed over the boundary into interstellar space on December 10, 2018. [15]

That's 41 years later. Now, lest you think of it as drifting at a slow speed like that of a nervous driver chugging along in the far-right lane of an interstate thruway, think again. Its speed was clocked at about **35,000 miles per hour!** And it still took **41 years!!** One more, and we're done.

The next closest star to our solar system is called Proxima Centauri. It is part of the Alpha Centauri star system and is 4.24 light years away. [16]

To put that distance in its proper perspective, think about some event in your life that occurred a little over four years ago. It doesn't happen quite like this in space, but imagine a light being turned on from Proxima Centauri when that personal event of yours took place. With light traveling at the speed of **186,000 miles per <u>second,</u>** it would just be getting here as you read this sentence...**from 4 years ago!!! ***And that's the CLOSEST star!!!!!** I don't know about you, but I'm finished!

When we reach a point where our finite minds are blown and we can't process the unthinkable, our human nature just has us throwing up our hands and disengaging our imaginations. We then turn our thoughts over to more conceivable things like everyday concerns and mundane logic. It's enough to spend time contemplating the intricacies of the human body, and another to try to imagine how vast space is, but then how do we begin to realize that God is beyond the extremities of ALL dimensions? We can't. It's great that although He is so vast and is seated in heaven, He still makes our heart His home, and calls Himself our Father (II Corinthians 6:18).

The 23rd and 91st Psalms are all too familiar to many of us. But when I am reflecting on how awesome God and His creation are, I call on Psalm 8 to take me to a place of total appreciation. It's from that passage that I meditate effectively on how He has brought all things into existence and even wanted you and me to be a part of it. We may be but a speck in the fullness of His handiwork, but we are huge in His eyes. The moon, the stars, the suspension of astronomical spheres and masses that cannot be numbered; beyond all time, space, and matter, <u>we</u> matter...to Him!

This is the Father I had been searching and longing for, inadvertently. Earthly fathers are not to be forsaken because they are the initial vessels through which reproduction is achieved. Besides that, dads are supposed to replicate (of course, on a smaller scale) our Divine Overseer Who carries the weight of the world on His shoulders. In dad's case, though, the "world" should be his family. But it stands to reason that unless he looks to God to be his weight-bearer, he won't be fully conditioned to lead, safeguard, and love his family to his fullest ability.

My Remorse

I have wasted so much time and energy distressing over being father-less, when I should have focused more on the Father Who has **never** left me - and He will never leave me. Which brings me to my second apology. I beg God's forgiveness for looking past Him as the best Dad I could ever have. He has ordered my steps long before I was able to walk. His grace is beyond amazing, and no words describe it adequately. I am so thankful for His patience that in His omniscience He knew I would come around eventually. The Lord's shield has always been much more than a surface covering; it guarded the inner parts of me as well. I can recall multiple times along the way when I stood dumbfounded after being pulled from a dangerous situation that was no match for the Lord's defense.

I have looked back after the fact and thought, "That was nothing less than God's mercy at work." Several accounts have already been mentioned in the preceding chapters. (If any of you can attest to that, why not take a moment to think about it and give Him thanks?) And then, His provisions. In addition to the bare necessities and extra blessings, He gave our mother everything she needed to fill any cracks in our foundation. Through Him, she went way above, beyond, beside, and behind to teach us the right way to do things. Was she perfect? Of course not, but she was perfectly devoted to seeing us through thick and thin, and she made sure that we found our way. Again, forgive me, Lord, and thank You.

The SWOK Club

Hopefully, at this juncture we've put a few things into their proper place and now we have a more profound image of the God of all our "gaze." By better appreciating how He carefully made us, it should be easier to understand that He wants the best **for** us and **from** us. Learning what that is at an early age is not always possible, but we gain a great advantage if we can. Enter the SWOK Club!

SWOK is an acronym for *Stay With Our Kids*. It originated from a conversation many years ago with me and a couple of good-natured boys (ages 8 and 13). Somehow, we got around to talking about how the three of us felt about not growing up with a dad in the household. Since they were much younger than me, theirs was a fresh wound that required more attention. I listened to them and was heartbroken to see them both getting teary-eyed as they spoke. The 13-year-old (who happened to be my nephew) told of how his grandfather was absent from his father's life also. The profound statement he made was when he said, "The tradition stops here!" That gave me a flashback of that day I promised God the same thing when I was a boy. It was a very revealing chat we had, and we ended up spinning it in a positive direction.

I went on to explain how their fathers didn't leave because they didn't want to be with them. Either they left because they weren't ready for a family, or—as in a lot of cases—they just grew apart from your mothers. When I asked if they were up for examining some ways that might help them prevent their kids from going through the same thing when they become older, they jumped on board immediately. With that, we started meeting regularly, and the group grew from two boys to six boys that were all eager to relate to each other whose scenarios met at the same crossroad.

We had group chats, one-on-one discussions, Bible studies, recreational activities, and a week-long convention each summer. One of our funnest (Is that a word? Well, with them it was) things we did during the convention was our "Stay up Late" contest. We'd gather our favorite junk foods and grab a few movies to pop in the VCR. While watching late-night movies, we'd also be watching each other.

Whoever was caught falling asleep was dismissed (much like musical chairs) and would have to go to bed. As the eldest contestant, I'd always be among the first to drop off. Little did they know that I didn't mind a bit since my bedtime wasn't much past 9pm anyway.

All those things we did were great, but we really got into the nuts and bolts of what becoming a man should look like and how to select a wife with good character and qualities, and who is equally yoked. When that happens, walking away from your family is not even the slightest consideration. My message to them was that in order to **get** "quality" you must **bring** quality. So, we focused on things like good hygiene, conversation, manners, ambition, and thoughtfulness, just to name a few.

These elements, when using biblical principles to support them, were a good starting point. Many of us go right to the 31st chapter of Proverbs to find the perfect example of a virtuous woman. However, we usually zero-in on verses 10 thru 31 without noticing what's going on in verses 1-9. There you'll find a **mother** teaching her son how to be a virtuous **man**. Not only did that hit home, but it was a great place for my SWOK buddies to camp out.

Yes, according to God's original plan, women were called on to be the man's helper - (Lord knows we need it) but it doesn't mean that she is subservient to him. Although being loved by her is a beautiful thing, **adorning** him is different from **adoring** him. Under God's plan the man is supposed to be the head, and if that head is on straight, then she is to be the crown! Also, if bowing down to him is what he's after, then let's put a different spin on the imagery. If he's building her up, showing his appreciation for her, and his love for her has put her on a pedestal, then her bowing down is the only way they can meet at eye level! Call it mushy if you want and view it as unrealistic, but it's a lot closer to the way God designed it than it is to the mess that it has become throughout the generations. Each must do their part. It's not a give-and-take, it's a give-and-give. That way, everybody wins! Even at their young ages the SWOK guys got it, and we had big fun with our exclusive club.

These are just some of the innumerous wonders to behold. The longer we live, the more we see. The more we see, the clearer it becomes to us that we all have a Dad Who loves us, and we can't fully fathom the magnitude of His Fatherhood!

11

Spreading the Love

Okay, one last homework assignment before dismissal. This first part is only for parents who are raising their child or children singlehandedly. At the next opportune moment that is convenient for you and yours, bring them beside you and read the following message to them:

Single Moms

You may not know it, but you have been blessed with a "Super Parent." She has patterned herself after a virtuous woman who sacrifices all she can in order to give you the very best life possible. She thinks about you and prays for you constantly while asking God for His strength to carry her as she carries you. No mom is perfect, but she is perfectly willing to find every way imaginable to help you grow into the person that you were called to be. Her love may not be something you can physically touch, but it can touch **you**.

When it does, your heart will dance with excitement because it knows that her love is real and unconditional. It is understandable that she may grow weary from the added labor she has to undertake due to the absence of your dad. It's during those times that she will be energized by something special from you such as a hug, a kiss, a smile, a card, or an extra chore or favor. Even an "I love you" or "Thank you for all you do" would mean more to her than you could ever imagine. To you it may seem small, but to her it's the boost she needs to recharge herself so that she can push through.

Your mom is amazing. God used her to bring you life, and now He is using her to **enrich** your life. Please don't take her for granted, as she is doing the best that she can. When it's all over, you will be the fruit of her labor, and all her efforts will have been worth it because her beauty will be on display for the world to see through the beautiful person that you will become. Now, give her that smile and that hug, and go thank your Heavenly Father for giving her to you!

Single Moms, you are extra precious and loved more than you'll ever know!

<u>Single Dads</u>

You've seen plenty of Super Stars and Superheroes out there, but you are under the care of a real "Super Dad." There may be several reasons why he may be raising you by himself, but the important thing to know is that he is an awesome man because he loves you so much that he has gladly accepted an uncommon role. Smothering you with the kind of warmth that a nurturing mom offers so freely comes naturally for her, but a man must learn it and develop it.

As he does, he will add those qualities to the ones he already has as a father who guards you and provides for you. While you're being patient with him, please cherish him because he stands tall among the tallest men for his faithfulness to the Lord for the privilege of being your dad and teaching you all you need to know so that you can become a wonderful person.

If he ever seems tired, lonely, or confused, go to him and tell him or show him how much he is loved and appreciated by you. It will make him very happy and it will enable him to continue giving you the very best of himself as he leads you into adulthood. If you're a boy, watch dad closely and strive to be just like him when you become a man. If you're a girl, remember him in his loving ways and look for someone with qualities like his when you become a woman.

He is your "Super Dad" now and always, but don't forget your Ultimate Dad, Who is the Heavenly Father Who gave your dad his strength so that he could use it to be all that he can be for you!

Single dads, you deserve a standing ovation!!!

*This portion of the homework is a personal reading assignment for those falling under the highlighted categories:

Feel-Good Dads

You may or may not have felt a sense of pride when you first learned that you were going to be a dad. But it's likely that when the baby was born you were mesmerized by the tiny person who was a product of your biological system. It used to be traditional for the new dad to hand out cigars, stick out his chest, and be granted extended visiting hours in the maternity ward. It might not be the same way now, but it's evident that what **hasn't** changed much is the initial gratification brandished shortly after the birth of your child. Like anything else, the exuberance sort of fades as the responsibilities of being a father overtakes the joy you had when you were told initially that you were going to become one. But it usually resurfaces on a day called Father's Day.

Most dads should certainly be celebrated on that day, even though not all of them are worthy of recognition. They are the ones who feel good about the glory part of it, but not about the "gory" part that entails everything that has to do with the work involved in contributing towards the proper upbringing of their kids. This is not a condemnation against dads who want to be active in their children's lives but are sometimes faced with strong opposition from the mothers of the kids. In those cases, they should be as relentless as possible in trying to find a way to keep a connection with their children.

The main thing for "Feel-Good" dads to understand is that kids need to feel good about knowing that their father loves them enough to pursue a relationship with them. Children don't have a special day to be celebrated because theirs is an ongoing, demanding recognition that is often hard to satisfy. In time, the reward will make it all worthwhile. For now, **feel good** about knowing that any heartaches they may experience along life's journey should have nothing to do with your not being there for them when they needed you.

Real Good Dads

Somewhere out there, a football team has gathered before a big game to review several videos of their opponents' previous games. Every intricate detail of that team's offense and defense is played repeatedly so that they can spot predictable patterns which can help to develop strategies that will hopefully aid in winning the game. Although there are assistant coaches available to help instruct the players, it's the head coach who bears the burden of leading the team to victory.

Somewhere else, there's a devoted dad coaching his children on how to win the game of life. Just like that football team's head coach, he spends unlimited time with his "players" pointing out the opponent's tactics. He is up against an evil adversary who wants to not only defeat his children but wants to destroy them altogether. If he is the type of dad who still trusts God's plan, then he'll use the best playbook there is, the Bible.

There are many parents who are awesome people with good values and lots of integrity, but they are still at a disadvantage because they might not be using the same "playbook" to beat the enemy at his own game. The "opponent" is bent on using any instrument of trickery to confuse and disillusion those kids so that when they grow to be adults they are not only confounded, but they are also of little (if any) help to all who are looking to them for guidance.

The "Real Good" dad's sleeves are rolled up and he's down in the trenches with his kids. He's fun and creative yet he does not hesitate when correction is needed. He is tireless when it comes to going all out for his children, even when they have families of their own. These dads are out there; we all applaud you for being men of honor, integrity, and a template for generations of young men to emulate.

Stepdads

We've often assumed that the "step" portion of the title was put in place as the verb to describe what a man did when he married a woman with a child or children he didn't sire. I recently learned that it derived from the Old English word *Steop* which meant orphan. But the way in which many of us use the term is to see it as stepping in to fill a void left in a child's life by a father who is not around anymore. It doesn't always mean that dad walked away. In sad cases dad has **passed** away (as we saw in Tammy's situation). Since an orphan is defined as a child whose parents are deceased, its definition of origin (*Steop*) doesn't seem very fitting. For that reason, let's stick with our own application of the word.

Stepfathers are more common these days after a couple has divorced. Because of the emotional aftermath of such a misfortune, it is often as difficult for him to adapt to the new arrangement as it is for the children. He walks into a family who have functioned as a unit before his arrival and must learn all its members and how they operate. The more pliable stepdad adjusts to the climate and settles into the groove as he is accepted in a role he chose to—as they say—"sign up for." The best-case scenario is when he and the family inadvertently discard the "step" and are happily left with just plain ol' "dad." These awesome men are in the hero group as well because of their ability to love the kids unconditionally and take on any challenges that come his way.

It pains my heart to say that I don't think I did a very good job as a member of this category. Coming into it without healing from not experiencing the joy and novelty of seeing a baby born from my own genetics was a major drawback. Add to that the disadvantage of not having any fatherly guidance to teach me how to operate as a dad, and it became easy to see how I may have failed to be a comfort to my wife's three adolescent children. My expectations were unfair, my skin was too thin, and my maturity level was too low. There were never any explosive situations, ever. But I still don't think I measured up to what many other stepdads brought into their families. Those are the true heroes of this group.

Keep steppin' dads.You've earned much love and respect from a community of admirers who hold you in high esteem for your selflessness!

A "MAD" (Mom and Dad) Household

That acronym is a misrepresentation of this preferred type of household. You folks are just as much heroes as the rest because a shifting culture and social media influences have made it harder for you to stay together. Now, more than ever, you need all the help you can get to weather the storms of adversity. Apparently, you've found a certain cohesiveness that is not sold in Home Improvement stores. You still have all the trials within your walls as any other family, but one less thing you have to encounter is the sting of an absent parent. Still, you're challenged by so many rules and definitions that are changing faster than you can blink.

Unfortunately, we're living at a time when role designations and policies are spinning in a whirlpool of confusion. So, a lot of persons may not see a mom and dad as key components in terms of a sustainable way to solidify the family structure. The honorable standards that we once lived by are either mocked, ignored, or redefined to support the profuse assortment of shifting winds swirling around us. What was good is now bad, and what was bad is now good.

Remarkably, many people know this, but peer pressures from all ages have contributed to a willingness to compromise so as not to look like the oddball. Especially now, it's time to return to the rule book-God's Rule Book. We used to trust Him enough to attempt to live by it. Now, it's tossed aside like an outdated magazine with stale information that doesn't apply to today's way of doing things. As a result—chaos. The following is a somewhat comical (yet, true) example of how rules are arbitrarily changed to suit the counter-cultural movements and agendas that are plaguing our society:

I was sitting and relaxing on a playground bench one day watching a group of about six little boys who were engaged in a game of Tag. Another youngster, who was a stranger to them, approached them and asked if he could play.

The biggest guy (clearly the leader) said, "Yeah, but you have to be 'It'."

The new player agreed, and the chase began. He was a fast runner, so it didn't take long for him to run down one of the slower players and put a tag on him. Instead of the captured runner becoming "It", which is according to the universal rules of the game, the leader said, "You can't tag him; he's too little."

It was the funniest thing when that new player looked at me, knowing that I was a witness to what was going on, shrugged his shoulders as if to say, *Oh, well,* then began to chase the pack again. He zeroed in on the leader and ran him down almost as easily as he did his first victim.

Just as he was about to tag him, the guy said, "Time."

He went on to say, "I called time before you tagged me."

Seriously?! The game resumed and this time he tagged another boy who neglected to call time. Ready for this?

The leader then said, "Now you have to catch ALL of us!" I jumped up off that bench and went into the mix looking like the giant from "Gulliver's Travels."

I said, "Wait a minute. You can't keep changing the rules!"

I took control of the game by telling the newly tagged player, "You're It now," then I sat back down to watch a more fair and organized game of Tag!

Back to you, parents. I encourage you to continue playing by the rules. Rules were also given to the original couple in the Garden of Eden. Those "players" didn't obey the rules, which is why mankind became flawed and has been bearing the brunt of their fall ever since then. Teach your children to honor God's rules and resist every temptation to sway from them.

Mom and Dad, you rock! Great job!

***

Most of us would probably think we still trust and depend on God to meet us at our points of need, but do we trust Him to lead us in the right paths? Sadly, times have changed radically over the years to where we don't even think of Him, much less lean on the Bible for instructions on how we should live our lives.

Instead of the "In God We Trust" statement which we used to display proudly, more aptly the question should be, "Can God Trust Us?" Can He trust us to follow the rules He has put before us? If we're honest, we can look around and see that the answer is a resounding, **"No."**

So, if we can't trust a Heavenly Father to lead us, how in the world can we trust an earthly father to lead?

As it pertains to the dire need for fathers to return to good parental practices and embrace their obligation to lead their children, it all comes down to what's beneath the surface of their being. In other words, **the heart of the matter is a matter of the heart**. It's what's in there that will be revealed via how much of himself he gives his kids.

The accent is on the importance of father-to-son training because of the continuation of the leadership role. However, it is no less imperative for dad to smother his daughter with his love and attention so that she has a firm grip on her worth and how crucial his example is when it comes time for her to choose between those "contestants" who will be competing for her admiration later.

Our Supreme Dad doesn't necessarily need an earthly father to lead the crusade for a return to the rules, but since He put man in a position to help guide the first children that ever existed, why not restore His faith in us to pioneer a migration from the passive comfort zones to which we've grown accustomed? Your children need you, dad.

They need you, even with all your imperfections, apprehensions, and uncertainties. Just **be** there. First, answer the door of your heart when the Greatest Dad of all, knocks. Then, both of you go together and knock on the door that has separated you from those children for too long.

Finally, your mission will be an anointed one, and your prize will be waiting for you with open arms, tears of joy, and the whisper of "Well Done" from the One Who will never leave **you** as you never leave them!

Prayer for Healing

D ear Lord,

You are Supreme over all that ever was, is, and ever will be.

Grant us access to Your throne room

that we might be heard within the splendor of your fullness.

You are the One Who stands as the Father of all Fathers.

Moreover, You are a Father to the fatherless.

We pray for a special touch of healing and grace to cover those who have been deeply wounded by the absence of an earthly dad.

We understand unavoidable circumstances that prevented some fathers from being present, and we take a step of obedience to forgive the others who left without cause.

In all cases, gather the morsels of brokenness and sow them over the field of souls who are in dire need of healing.

Then, may You reap a harvest of fresh, vibrant men ready and eager to do the work of helping to build Your kingdom on earth, as it is in heaven.

Gather into place these men of plan and purpose and raise them up so that they may raise up more behind them.

May all dads heed the cry of Your voice calling them to a higher ground of faithfulness,

where You will meet them and give them hope for a glistening future.

We pray in advance for those who may scoff at the convicting insights of this message,

and ask that a fresh desire to seek and serve You will stir within the hearts of dads who have become nomads in a land of temporal pleasures.

If but only one will change his course and become a prodigal dad returning home,

You will be the Dad Who runs to meet him, embrace him and say, "Welcome back, dad. Your children await you with forgiving hearts and will be so glad to see you."

Lord, please attend to the men who have longed to become dads but haven't been able.

Theirs is an indescribable pain that many do not understand.

These men are hidden in the crevices of a place of suffering as life goes on around them.

At every bend in the road is a constant reminder of what they may never experience.

Comfort may be beyond their reach, but the closeness of Your hand brings relief to the hurting.

Finally, forgive us as we have so often forgotten that You are our Heavenly Father.

You are the Dad who **never** leaves us or forsakes us.

During these troubled days of turmoil all around, no agendas or movements can prevail against the movement of Your Holy Spirit.

Make it so that more eyes would see, more ears would hear, and more hearts would feel Your insatiable love through the sacrificial life that Jesus laid down for us on the cross.

As the light of mortality dims, brighter shines the light of a blissful eternity with You in a new heaven and earth.

Hear our prayer, Lord,

And grant our desires according to Your will.

With much love and thanksgiving, we pray...

Amen.

Acknowledgments

A special thank you to the lady of my life. My wife Catherine is my soulmate, coach, and biggest fan, all wrapped up in one. Her confidence in my ability to complete this project has been the driving force behind every doubtful moment that tried to discourage me. I thank God for her, and for her believing in me every step of the way.

She is also the brains behind the technical and administrative aspects of all creative notions that I dare to entertain. Thank you, Cathy. I love you and applaud you for being with me throughout this brand-new leg of our journey together!

Thanks to my friends and family who have allowed me to share their personal trials and triumphs through the heartfelt agonies of journeying without dad. Your courageous input has been greatly appreciated and is certain to play a part in the impact that this book will have on its readers.

So grateful for my longtime friend James Fleet, who many years ago said, "Yes you can," when I said, "I can't." His amazing artwork has been featured in multiple print materials over the years, and I am honored to have partnered with him in several creative adventures in the past. Thanks again, James. You will always be my friend and favorite artist!

A special thanks to my precious nieces, Leah and Shakira. They are the catalysts who launched the search to find Denise and me, as a gift to their mother, Cheryl. In doing so, they united us with our long-lost sister and brother (Cheryl and Charles) and enhanced our family by showing us what drive and determination can deliver. Without their knowing it, they have inspired me to press ahead and get this book written.

Michelle G. Cameron is my editor who has come alongside to not only instruct, but to bring a professionalism lavished by the nature of the Lord. Her contribution to the publication of this book has given it the substance and appeal to reach many readers, as well as those authors out there who need her expertise to help them get started. Thanks so much, Michelle. You are a gifted tutor with a selfless heart for showing all writers how to reach new heights. So blessed to have you in our lives!

Last, but far from least, thank you Pastor Mike for your prayers of intercession and words of wisdom. Your trusted persuasion stirred my faith and gave me the confidence to believe that it was time to retire from full-time employment and allow God to lead me into a new and exciting season. You are my brother, my friend, and another fine example of what authentic fatherhood looks like.

***

References

1. **Chapter 5:** Russ. (2021, August 10). *How does the eye work? - Optometrists.org*. Optometrists.org. https://www.optometrists.org/general-practice-optometry/guide-to-eye-health/how-does-the-eye-work/

2. **Chapter 6:** Writing Explained. (2017, June 8). *What Does There But For The Grace Of God Go I Mean? - Writing Explained.* https://writingexplained.org/idiom-dictionary/there-but-for-the-grace-of-god-go-i

3. **Chapter 8:** Nel, P. (2021, August 31). *Horatio Gates Spafford - The story behind the hymn "It is well with my soul" — Bethel Church Ripon.* Bethel Church Ripon. https://www.bethelripon.com/life-stories/horatio-gates-spafford

4. **Chapter 10:** *Speed of sperm per hour - Google Search.* (n.d.). https://www.google.com/search?client=safari&sca_esv=576501417&hl=en-us&sxsrf=AM9HkKk7Nj7qd-rytnUKKrk99A35VY4CCg:1698242220586&q=Speed+of+sperm+per+hour&sa=X&ved=2ahUKEwjStbOirZGCAxUtJkQIHTOTDJIQ1QJ6BAg_EAI&biw=462&bih=872&dpr=3

5. **Chapter 10:** Dunkin, M. A. (2010, September 7). *Sperm FAQ.* WebMD. https://www.webmd.com/infertility-and-reproduction/sperm-and-semen-faq

6. **Chapter 10:** Fertility, N. I. (2021, August 25). How long does it take for a sperm to fertilize an egg? *Nova IVF Fertility.*

https://www.novaivffertility.com/fertility-help/how-long
-does-it-take-for-a-sperm-to-fertilize-an-egg

7. **Chapter 10:** Professional, C. C. M. (n.d.). *Fetal development*. Cleveland Clinic.
https://my.clevelandclinic.org/health/articles/7247-fetal-d
evelopment-stages-of-growth

8. **Chapter 10:** Department of Health & Human Services. (n.d.). *Muscles*. Better Health Channel.
https://www.betterhealth.vic.gov.au/health/conditionsand
treatments/muscles#

9. **Chapter 10:** Department of Health & Human Services. (n.d.-a). *Bones*. Better Health Channel.
https://www.betterhealth.vic.gov.au/health/conditionsand
treatments/bones#

10. **Chapter 10:** Russ. (2021, August 10). *How does the eye work? - Optometrists.org*. Optometrists.org.
https://www.optometrists.org/general-practice-optometry
/guide-to-eye-health/how-does-the-eye-work/

11. **Chapter 10:** *Heart facts Infographic*. (n.d.). American Heart Association.
https://newsroom.heart.org/file?fid=59a7145e2cfac2546c
ae1995

12. **Chapter 10:** British Heart Foundation. (n.d.). How do new blood vessels grow. *British Heart Foundation*. Retrieved October 24, 2023, from
https://www.bhf.org.uk/informationsupport/heart-matte
rs-magazine/research/how-are-blood-vessels-made

13. **Chapter 10:** Lung Foundation Australia. (2022, December

9). *How your lungs work - Lung Foundation Australia.*
https://lungfoundation.com.au/lung-health/protecting-yo
ur-lungs/how-your-lungs-work

14. **Chapter 10:** Byju's. (2022, July 4). *How many earths can be
fit inside the sun-.*
https://byjus.com/question-answer/how-many-earths-can
-be-fit-inside-the-sun-around-50000-around-500-around-1

15. **Chapter 10:** *Voyager 2 - NASA Science.* (n.d.).
https://science.nasa.gov/mission/voyager-2/

16. **Chapter 10:** *Proxima Centauri | star.* (n.d.). Encyclopedia
Britannica.
https://www.britannica.com/science/Proxima-Centauri